D0852287

LAURA
IN THE
KITCHEN

LAURA
IN THE
KITCHEN

Favorite Italian-American
Recipes Made Easy

LAURA VITALE

PHOTOGRAPHS BY LUCY SCHAEFFER

Clarkson Potter/Publishers
New York

FOR MY NONNA, who is my biggest
inspiration, both in and out of the kitchen

Published in the United States by Clarkson Potter/
Publishers, an imprint of the Crown Publishing
Group, a division of Penguin Random House LLC,
New York.
www.crownpublishing.com
www.clarksonpotter.com

CLARKSON POTTER is a trademark and POTTER
with colophon is a registered trademark of
Penguin Random House LLC.

Library of Congress Cataloging-in-Publication Data
Vitale, Laura, 1986–
    Laura in the kitchen : favorite Italian-American
recipes made easy / Laura Vitale ; photographs by
Lucy Schaeffer. —First edition.
        pages   cm
    Includes index.
    1. Cooking, Italian. 2. Cooking, American.
I. Title.
    TX723.V565 2015
    641.5945—dc23   2015009570

ISBN 978-0-8041-8713-8
Ebook ISBN 978-0-8041-8714-5

Printed in United States of America

Book and cover design: La Tricia Watford
Cover photography: Lucy Schaeffer

10 9 8 7 6 5 4 3 2 1

First Edition

CONTENTS

WELCOME TO MY KITCHEN   7

PANTRY BASICS   10

QUICK-FIX SUPPERS   17

LEISURELY ENTRÉES   69

SUPER-SIMPLE SALADS & SIDES 119

IRRESISTIBLE DESSERTS   148

THE COOKIE JAR   181

EASY BREAKFASTS & BRUNCHES   201

ACKNOWLEDGMENTS   236

INDEX   237

WELCOME TO
MY KITCHEN

W as it the aroma of garlic and tomatoes that tempted you here? On the weekend I do like to have a pot of marinara simmering on the stove. Join me for an espresso. The lemon almond biscotti will be out of the oven and ready for dunking, presto!

If it's Sunday, I'm doing what I love to do best—filling my home with food for family and friends, and for the week ahead. Come Monday, my routine changes. Between work and family, I'm on the go all week, so I need dishes that are ready in a flash. But don't worry: I'll let you in on all of my secrets in this book, including how a girl from a small town in Italy started her own cooking show on YouTube.

HOW IT ALL BEGAN

I grew up in southern Italy, near Naples, cooking alongside my nonna—my grandmother. When I moved to the United States at age twelve to live with my father, I was desperately homesick. My nonna told me to stop feeling sorry for myself. "Cook a pot of sauce," she advised. So I did. And I felt a little better. On the phone, she talked me through all the recipes we used to prepare together so that I could cook them in New Jersey and make this new place feel a bit more like home. Ever since then, even though my nonna remains an ocean away, I've sensed her by my side at the stove.

I've been cooking almost as long as I've been eating, from those early days in Italy to working in my father's pizzeria beginning in my teens. In fact, when his restaurants closed suddenly, I found myself not only without a job, but also without a purpose. Joe and I were engaged at the time, and so, thankfully, I started working at his family's business, a succulent-plant distributor. I became a cactus expert! I filled orders, packed them, arranged the tractor-trailers to deliver them, and became the bookkeeper. I was happy to have a job, but I knew deep down that I really wanted to be cooking instead. And I *really* wanted to write a cookbook.

Just as my nonna told me to make a pot of sauce, Joe told me to start my own cooking show. If people liked it, *then* maybe I could write a cookbook. He even volunteered to help, and in 2009 we turned our empty basement into a little studio that I could cook in. *Laura in the Kitchen* was born.

Now, with hundreds of recipes shared first on YouTube and now also on my Cooking Channel program, I continue to do what I love and love what I do. The most rewarding part has been hearing from fans, that I helped them get over their fear of the kitchen and become passionate about feeding their loved ones. My aim has never been to teach my viewers how to be "perfect" chefs because, let's face it, *I'm* no perfect chef! Instead, it's about sharing my love for the kitchen and the pure joy and pleasure it can bring. I hope to inspire you to feel the same way.

And now, finally, I've done what I was waiting to do all along: write a cookbook. Here are recipes that combine the influence of my southern Italian home—red sauces, oregano, basil, garlic, sweet and hot peppers, lemons, ricotta, and lots of pasta—with my American palate. I like to put an Italian spin on so many American and international specialties, including meat loaf, fattoush salad, chili, Greek meatballs, enchiladas and quesadillas, quiche, and more.

This book is a chance to put my most cherished recipes in print so that you can easily cook along with me at home. Almost all of the recipes are new and can't be found elsewhere, though I have included a handful of absolute favorites from my website to keep everyone happy. (Yes, my red velvet cupcakes are in here.)

HOW TO USE THIS BOOK

While work, family, errands, laundry, and a list of chores as long as your arm can make cooking on a weeknight seem like a distant priority, it doesn't have to be. In fact, I find it's on the hectic days that I most need the comfort of a home-cooked meal. Other than the occasional night when we're invited out or when I'm traveling, you'll find me in my kitchen preparing dinner for Joe and me. That's when I turn to my recipes for Quick-Fix Suppers, like Calamari Puttanesca and Ciabatta Steak Sandwich with Arugula. I know I can get a good, from-scratch meal on the table with little time and effort, and that the time we take together to eat will help us both unwind.

When the weekend rolls around, I follow my Italian tradition of relaxing at home with family and friends. It's a time to slow down in the kitchen, too, putting platter after platter of family-style dishes like Tagliatelle with Mushroom Ragù and Garlic-Stuffed Pork Loin on the table for those I love. My Leisurely Entrées take a bit more time to develop their deep, soulful flavors, but they're not at all difficult. Plus, unless you're feeding a crowd, most will leave you with leftovers to enjoy for lunches or dinners throughout the week.

With a hearty entrée made fast or slow, all you need is a quick bit of color and contrast—like Cumin-Roasted Carrots or Sautéed Garlic & Lemon Zucchini—to round out your meal. Super-Simple Salads & Sides give you everything you need to transform a simple main dish into a full dinner. Some, like Panzanella Salad, can even be served as a light meal on their own.

My nonna taught me that no self-respecting Italian would serve a meal without dessert. Turn to Irresistible Desserts when you want to make any meal feel like a special occasion. This chapter includes family favorites, such as a Stunning Pavlova mounded with whipped cream and berries and a deeply decadent Devilishly Good Devil's Food Cake that has a devoted following on my website. For sweets that are ready when friends drop by, look no further than the humble Cookie Jar. Here, you'll find treats like Fig Jam Cookies and Fudgy Brownies to have on hand for guests—or when your own sweet tooth strikes.

At my house, weekday breakfasts are a quick affair: a muffin or a handful of granola and a cup of coffee grabbed on the way out the door. When the weekend rolls around, I'm ready to indulge in Easy Breakfasts & Brunches, such as Cheddar-Bacon Waffles or Italian Eggs Benedict or the ultimate sweet morning treat: Homemade Italian Doughnuts. Many of the recipes in this chapter can be prepped the night before, making it easy to finish and serve them without spoiling your relaxing Saturday or Sunday morning.

The key to easily and efficiently turning out flavorful food lies in properly setting up your kitchen. Make the foundation recipes in Pantry Basics and you're halfway there. Having Pesto and Marinara Sauce on hand, whether in the fridge or freezer, means you're only a box of pasta away from a last-minute meal. I am all about simplicity: If I can't find an ingredient at a local store or easily online, I'm not going to spend my time hunting it down. I am rarely attached to a specific brand, but where I think it makes a difference, I mention my preferences in the individual recipes.

I hope my recipes fill your kitchen with the same comfort and joy they do mine, and that you share that good food and feeling with the people you love most. Follow me—let's cook!

PANTRY BASICS

My well-stocked pantry has me ready to put a great meal on the table at a moment's notice. For the most part, I use the basic equipment and ingredients almost everyone has on hand: a quality set of pots and pans, nonstick skillets in a few sizes, a standing mixer, a food processor, and, of course, a set of good, sharp knives. I keep basic ingredients in my pantry that suit my Italian-American palate, with a few ingredients from around the world for those times when I want a change of pace. (I can eat Italian almost every day, so that's not often!)

Once a month, I take an inventory of my pantry, freezer, and fridge, making a list of items I'm running low on. With list in hand, I make my big monthly shopping trip, stocking up on kitchen basics. In between those monthly outings, all I need to pick up is fresh produce and other perishables specific to the recipes I have in mind, making shopping a breeze.

PANTRY

OLIVE OIL
extra-virgin, for when the flavor will really stand out, and regular (often labeled "pure")

SAFFLOWER OIL

DRIED HERBS AND SPICES
such as dried oregano and basil, cumin, chili powder, granulated onion and garlic, and crushed red pepper flakes

TABLE SALT

CANNED TOMATOES
in a few varieties, such as *passata*, crushed tomatoes, and whole plum tomatoes

CANNED BEANS
such as black beans, cannellini, and chickpeas

DRIED PASTA
such as penne, linguini, and ditalini

RICE
such as Arborio, long grain, and brown

SOUP BASES
which take up less cabinet space than boxed stocks. I keep chicken, beef, and vegetable on hand.

CANNED TUNA
packed in water, and Italian tuna, packed in olive oil

BAKING PANTRY

ALL-PURPOSE FLOUR

ROLLED OATS

BAKING POWDER

BAKING SODA

ACTIVE DRY YEAST

CORNSTARCH

GRANULATED SUGAR

LIGHT BROWN SUGAR

PURE VANILLA EXTRACT

VANILLA BEANS or VANILLA PASTE

SEMISWEET CHOCOLATE CHIPS

REFRIGERATOR

PARMIGIANO-REGGIANO CHEESE
in blocks for grating (ditch the green can!)

UNSALTED BUTTER

HEAVY CREAM

CREAM CHEESE

VEGETABLE SHORTENING

ONIONS

GARLIC

LEMONS

FREEZER

ASSORTED BERRIES

PEAS

SPINACH

PUFF PASTRY

PIE CRUSTS

PIZZA DOUGH

ICE CREAM!

A FEW BASIC RECIPES

With the pantry items mentioned on page 11 and the handful of recipes that follow, you will always be ready to put dinner on the table at a moment's notice. Just boil your preferred pasta shape and heat some *passata* or marinara from the fridge or freezer. Toss the drained pasta with the sauce, adding a handful of fresh herbs, if you have them, or Italian seasoning to taste. Grate Parmigiano-Reggiano over the top and you're good to go—no recipe, no trouble. Not in the mood for red sauce? Use pesto in its place and skip the Italian seasoning. Cook this way once or twice and I guarantee you'll feel like an Italian kitchen pro in no time!

Marinara Sauce

This is my go-to, basic red sauce: I usually make a batch on Sunday to use throughout the week. The sauce keeps for up to a week in a glass jar in the fridge, or may be frozen for up to one month.

MAKES ABOUT 3 CUPS

3 tablespoons olive oil

1 small yellow onion, finely chopped

2 garlic cloves, minced

1 (28-ounce) can Italian plum tomatoes

1 teaspoon Italian seasoning, homemade (page 14) or store-bought

Salt and freshly ground black pepper

6 fresh basil leaves, torn

1   Put a 2-quart saucepan over medium heat. Add the oil, heat for a minute, then add the onion and cook until it softens and begins to color around the edges, 2 to 3 minutes. Add the garlic and cook for 1 minute longer.

2   Empty the tomatoes into a bowl and squeeze them with your hands to roughly crush them. (Don't be shy! This can be therapeutic.)

3   Add the tomatoes to the pot, along with the Italian seasoning. Reduce the heat to medium-low and let simmer for 20 minutes.

4   Season to taste with salt and pepper, and stir in the basil.

Tomato *Passata*

Passata is a purée of blanched tomatoes that is then strained to remove the skins and seeds. You may find it in glass jars in an Italian grocery, or in the supermarket aisle alongside the canned tomatoes. Pomì brand strained tomatoes are widely available. If you can't find a purée of nothing but tomatoes, here's how to make your own, using either canned or fresh tomatoes.

Refrigerate the *passata* in a glass jar for up to one week, or freeze in an airtight container for up to two months.

CANNED TOMATO METHOD (makes 2 cups): Pulse a 28-ounce can of whole or crushed tomatoes briefly in a food processor. Pass through a strainer, pressing firmly on the solids to extract as much tomato purée as possible. Discard the solids.

FRESH TOMATO METHOD (makes 2½ cups): Bring a pot of water to a boil. Add 2 pounds of plum tomatoes (about 8 medium tomatoes) and blanch for 2 minutes. Drain well, then pass the tomatoes through a food mill, or pulse them briefly in a food processor and pass through a strainer, pressing firmly on the solids to extract as much tomato purée as possible. Discard the solids.

This is the seasoning blend I return to over and over again in my recipes for authentic flavor that tastes like home to me. Store it in an airtight container away from heat and light for up to two months.

Italian Seasoning

2 tablespoons dried basil

2 tablespoons dried parsley

1 tablespoon dried oregano

1 tablespoon granulated garlic

2 teaspoons granulated onion

1 teaspoon dried rosemary

¼ teaspoon crushed red
    pepper flakes

Pulse all of the ingredients in a mini food processor just a couple of times, or crush them lightly with a mortar and pestle, to break them up and release their essential oils. Alternatively, crush the dried herbs by rubbing them between your palms.

I love to keep this vibrant green sauce on hand to stir into risotto (see page 48), to stuff chicken breasts (see page 51), or to toss with pasta for a simple meal.

For easy storage, I spoon the mixture into the wells of an ice cube tray, cover each with a film of olive oil, and freeze. Once they're frozen, I pop out the cubes and transfer them to a resealable plastic bag, where the pesto keeps well in the freezer for up to one month. That way I can take out what I need when I need it, without having to defrost the whole batch.

Basil Pesto

1 Heat an 8-inch skillet over medium heat. Add the pine nuts and toast until golden, about 3 minutes, shaking the pan occasionally to evenly toast them. Transfer the nuts to a plate and let cool completely.

2 Pulse the basil, garlic, lemon zest and juice, and nuts several times in a food processor. With the processor running, drizzle in the oil in a slow, steady stream until it forms a relatively smooth paste.

3 Transfer the pesto to a bowl and use a spatula to stir in the parmigiano. Season to taste with salt and pepper.

¼ cup pine nuts

2½ cups fresh basil leaves

2 garlic cloves

1 teaspoon finely grated lemon zest

1 teaspoon fresh lemon juice

½ cup extra-virgin olive oil

⅓ cup freshly grated Parmigiano-Reggiano

Salt and freshly ground black pepper

Weeknight Minestrone

Fresh Tomato Soup

Easy Butternut Squash Soup with Crispy Sage Leaves

Fattoush with Grilled Chicken

Greek Meatballs in Pita

Ciabatta Steak Sandwich with Arugula

Speedy Weeknight Cheeseburgers

Spaghetti Cacio e Pepe

Bow-Tie Pasta with Peas, Ham & Gorgonzola

Pasta Shells with No-Cook Tuna Sauce

Calamari Puttanesca

Tortellini with Pink Parmesan Sauce

Pasta alla Norma with Sausage Meatballs

Pasta with Chickpeas

Spaghetti Carbonara

QUICK-FIX SUPPERS

Quinoa Salad with Poached Salmon

Mock Risotto with Pesto & Turkey Marinara

Pasta e Fagioli

Pesto & Goat Cheese–Stuffed Chicken Breasts

Sausages with Black Lentils

Halibut Saltimbocca

Crispy Fish Cakes with Tartar Sauce

White Wine Mussels with Garlicky Bruschetta

Sausage & Clams with Tomatoes

One-Pan Chicken with Potatoes, Wine & Olives

Grilled Flank Steak with Chimichurri

Pork Chops alla Milanese

This is my speedy version of the classic Italian "big soup." The food processor does all the chopping and the stove does all the cooking, leaving little effort on your part. The soup will fill your kitchen with the most comforting aroma, perfect for the end of a hectic day.

Weeknight Minestrone

1 Pulse the onion, celery, and carrot in a food processor until they are very finely chopped.

2 Heat the olive oil in a large stockpot over medium-high heat until hot. Add the processed vegetables and a pinch of salt. Cook until the vegetables begin to cook down and take on a bit of color, about 5 minutes.

3 Add the broth, kidney beans, marinara, and Italian seasoning. Bring the mixture to a boil, then reduce the heat and simmer for 5 minutes.

4 Add the zucchini, green beans, and pasta. Cook until the pasta is al dente, about 10 minutes, stirring occasionally.

5 Remove the pot from the heat. Stir in the baby spinach and basil to wilt them. Add salt and pepper to taste.

6 Ladle the hot soup into bowls and top with freshly grated parmigiano.

1 small yellow onion, quartered

2 ribs celery, coarsely chopped

1 large carrot, coarsely chopped

3 tablespoons olive oil

6 cups low-sodium vegetable broth

1 (14.5-ounce) can kidney beans, rinsed and drained

1¼ cups marinara sauce, homemade (page 13) or store-bought

2 teaspoons Italian seasoning, homemade (page 14) or store-bought

1 large or 2 small zucchini, cut into ½-inch dice

2 cups green beans, trimmed and cut into ½-inch pieces

10 ounces (1¼ cups) small pasta, such as ditalini or conchigliette shells

2 cups baby spinach

5 fresh basil leaves, torn

Salt and freshly ground black pepper

Freshly grated Parmigiano-Reggiano

In midsummer, when tomatoes are candy-sweet and basil grows in abundance, there is no better use for them than this. The secret to this recipe lies in roasting the tomatoes to intensify their sweetness. If you have a powerful blender, such as a Vitamix or Blendtec, you can skip the straining step. With an immersion blender, you'll almost certainly need to strain it to get the desired velvety consistency. With soup this smooth, there's no need for even a touch of cream to mute its naturally sweet tomato flavor.

Fresh Tomato Soup

3 pounds plum tomatoes, halved

10 garlic cloves

2 large shallots, quartered

1 cup fresh basil, leaves and stems

¼ cup extra-virgin olive oil

1 tablespoon balsamic vinegar

2 teaspoons dried oregano

1 teaspoon sugar

Pinch of crushed red pepper flakes

Up to 1 cup low-sodium vegetable broth

Salt and freshly ground black pepper

1   Preheat the oven to 425°F.

2   Put the tomatoes, garlic, shallots, and basil into a 9 × 13-inch baking dish. Drizzle the oil and vinegar over the tomatoes, then sprinkle with the oregano, sugar, and pepper flakes. Toss everything together with your hands to evenly distribute the oil and seasonings.

3   Roast until the tomatoes have released most of their juices and the edges of everything appear caramelized, about 1 hour 15 minutes, tossing the tomatoes occasionally as they bake. Set aside to cool to room temperature.

4   Blend the cooled tomato mixture in a blender, or in a saucepan using an immersion blender, until completely smooth. For the silkiest soup, pass the soup through a fine-mesh strainer into a saucepan, pressing on the solids to extract as much soup as possible. Discard any bits remaining in the strainer. If not straining, transfer the soup directly to a saucepan.

5   Bring the soup just to a boil, then let it simmer to meld the flavors, about 5 minutes, adding broth, if needed, to achieve your desired texture. Season to taste with salt and pepper, and serve hot.

I sometimes think that lemony sage was created specifically for the purpose of complementing the earthy sweetness of butternut squash. When puréed, the squash has a velvety texture that makes it ideal for soup. I often top this soup with a few drops of chile oil for an extra hit of heat.

Easy Butternut Squash Soup with Crispy Sage Leaves

1   In a large soup pot, heat 2½ tablespoons of the oil over medium-high heat until hot. Add the squash, onion, celery, carrot, and apple and sauté until the vegetables are golden, 10 to 12 minutes. Add the chile powder and a small pinch of salt and cook for 30 seconds longer.

2   Add the broth and dried sage. Bring the mixture to a boil, then reduce the heat and simmer until the squash is very soft, about 40 minutes.

3   Working in batches, use a standard blender or food processor to make a smooth purée. (Alternatively, use an immersion blender right in the pot.)

4   Add salt and pepper to taste. Stir in the cream. Cover the soup and set aside off the heat.

5   Line a plate with paper towels. Heat the remaining 2 tablespoons oil in a small skillet until very hot. (When you drop in a sliver of sage leaf it should quickly sizzle and brown.) Add the sage all at once and cook, moving it around with a heat-proof spoon, until it turns brown and crispy, 1 to 2 minutes. Transfer the sage to the plate to drain.

6   To serve, ladle the hot soup into bowls and top with the crispy sage leaves.

4½ tablespoons olive oil

6 cups (1-inch) cubed peeled butternut squash

1 large yellow onion, coarsely chopped

2 ribs celery, coarsely chopped

1 carrot, coarsely chopped

1 large Granny Smith apple, peeled and coarsely chopped

1 teaspoon ancho chile powder

6 cups low-sodium vegetable broth

1 teaspoon dried sage

Salt and freshly ground black pepper

2 tablespoons heavy cream

8 fresh sage leaves, rolled together and cut into thin strips

This bread salad, from my Italian perspective, is the Middle Eastern version of panzanella—though I'm sure someone raised with this pita-based salad would call panzanella the Italian fattoush! Either way you look at it, it's loaded with large chunks of vegetables, plenty of fresh herbs, and crunchy pita, all tossed together in a lemony dressing. Served alongside grilled chicken, this salad makes a wonderfully simple summer dinner. If you prefer not to pound the chicken yourself, ask your butcher to prepare it "scaloppini style."

Za'atar is a Middle Eastern spice blend that typically includes oregano, thyme, sumac, and sometimes salt and sesame seeds. Look for it in the spice aisle of your supermarket or in stores that carry Middle Eastern ingredients, or do as I do: order it online.

Fattoush with Grilled Chicken

CHICKEN

4 chicken breasts (about 1¼ pounds), pounded thin

Finely grated zest and juice of ½ lemon

2 tablespoons olive oil

1 teaspoon granulated garlic

½ teaspoon chopped fresh thyme

Salt and freshly ground black pepper

SALAD

2 pita breads, split horizontally into 2 layers

¼ cup plus 2 tablespoons extra-virgin olive oil

2 teaspoons za'atar

1 small head romaine lettuce, finely chopped (about 6 cups)

1½ pounds ripe tomatoes, cut into large chunks

1 Marinate the chicken: Put the chicken in a bowl and sprinkle with the lemon zest and juice, oil, garlic, thyme, ¼ teaspoon salt, and a few grinds of pepper.

2 Meanwhile, start the salad: Preheat the oven to 400°F.

3 Brush both sides of the pita halves using 2 tablespoons of the oil and sprinkle both sides with 1 teaspoon of the za'atar. Arrange in a single layer on a baking sheet and bake until the pitas are just barely golden all over, 7 to 8 minutes. Let cool completely.

4 In a large bowl, toss together the lettuce, tomatoes, cucumber, scallions, parsley, and mint. Drizzle with the remaining ¼ cup oil, the lemon juice, and the remaining 1 teaspoon za'atar. Toss to evenly coat the vegetables with the dressing. Add salt and pepper to taste and toss again.

5 Heat a grill pan over medium-high heat. Grill the chicken until just cooked through, 2 to 3 minutes per side. Transfer the chicken to a plate and cover with foil to keep it warm.

6   Crumble 3 of the toasted pita halves into the salad and toss, allowing the pita to soak up some of the dressing.

7   To serve, divide the chicken among 4 plates. Crumble the final pita half over the top of the salad and then use tongs to mound the salad generously alongside the chicken. Sprinkle crumbled feta over the top, if using, and serve.

1 English cucumber, peeled and cut into 1-inch dice

4 scallions, white and light green parts only, chopped

½ cup coarsely chopped flat-leaf parsley

¼ cup coarsely chopped fresh mint

Juice of 1 lemon

Salt and freshly ground black pepper

Crumbled feta cheese (optional)

Flavored to the max and seared to perfection, these meatballs are perfect for tossing on a salad or, as I have here, stuffing into warm pita bread with the Greek cucumber-yogurt dip, tzatziki. I often finish mine with sliced tomato, a sprinkling of coarse sea salt, and sliced red onion.

Greek Meatballs in Pita

TZATZIKI

½ English cucumber

1½ cups 2% Greek yogurt

1 garlic clove, minced

Finely grated zest and juice of ½ lemon

Salt and freshly ground black pepper

MEATBALLS

1 cup fresh bread crumbs

¼ cup whole milk

1 large egg

2 tablespoons finely chopped fresh oregano

2 tablespoons finely chopped fresh mint

2 garlic cloves, minced

3 tablespoons grated yellow onion

½ teaspoon ground cumin

Finely grated zest of ½ lemon

½ teaspoon salt

Freshly ground black pepper

1½ pounds 85% lean ground beef or lamb

½ cup safflower oil

6 pita breads

1 Make the tzatziki: Grate enough of the cucumber to make ⅔ cup packed. Put the cucumber into a strainer and squeeze out as much liquid as possible, discarding the liquid. Transfer the cucumber to a bowl and stir in the yogurt, garlic, and lemon zest and juice. Add salt and pepper to taste. Cover with plastic wrap and refrigerate until serving time, or for up to 12 hours.

2 Make the meatballs: Put the bread crumbs into a small bowl and pour the milk over them. Let stand for a few minutes to allow the crumbs to soak up the milk.

3 In a large bowl, whisk together the egg, oregano, mint, garlic, onion, cumin, lemon zest, salt, and a few grinds of pepper. Stir in the meat and soaked bread crumbs and any milk remaining in the bowl until well mixed. Form the meat mixture into 24 walnut-size balls, putting them on a large plate as you form them. Cover the meatballs with plastic wrap and refrigerate for at least 30 minutes or up to several hours.

4 Preheat the oven to 375°F. Line a baking sheet with foil.

5 Put a large (approximately 10-inch) skillet over medium heat. Add the oil, heat for a minute, then add half of the meatballs to avoid crowding. Brown them just in a couple of spots, cooking them no more than about 4 minutes total. Transfer the seared meatballs to the prepared baking sheet as they are ready. Repeat with the remaining meatballs.

6 Bake the meatballs until they are cooked through to the center
   when you cut into one, 10 to 12 minutes. Let cool for 5 minutes.

7 Cut off the tops of the pitas and split them open. Tuck about
   4 meatballs into each pita, top them with tzatziki, and serve.

A giant sandwich using a whole loaf of ciabatta bread makes an impressive, yet easy meal for six. Pounding the steaks thin helps them to cook quickly, keeping them tender as they take on a hint of smoke from grilling. The steak juices mingle with olive oil, garlic, lemon, and parsley to infuse this genius sandwich with tons of flavor using only a few simple ingredients.

Ciabatta Steak Sandwich with Arugula

1 Put the steaks on a large cutting board. Cover them with plastic wrap and use a mallet or the bottom of a heavy skillet to pound them to an even thickness of about ¼ inch.

2 Season the steaks all over with salt and pepper. Drizzle them with 1½ tablespoons of the oil.

3 Preheat a grill pan over medium-high heat until hot.

4 Cut the ciabatta in half horizontally. Drizzle the remaining 1 tablespoon of oil over the cut sides, then put the halves, cut side down, on the pan, leaving them until they are well toasted with dark grill marks, 3 to 4 minutes. Transfer the bread to a plate (leave the pan on the heat) and immediately rub the toasted sides with the cut surfaces of the garlic.

5 Grill the steaks until medium rare, about 2½ minutes on each side. Transfer to a cutting board and let rest for 5 minutes.

6 Cut the steaks at a slight angle into thin strips, returning them and their juices to a bowl. Squeeze the lemon over the steaks, then sprinkle on the parsley and toss to coat.

7 To assemble the sandwich, pile the steak on the bottom half of the loaf and scatter arugula over the top. Drizzle the juices left in the bowl over everything, then cover with the top of the loaf. Cut the large sandwich crosswise into 6 pieces, and serve.

2 boneless rib-eye steaks (about 8 ounces each)

Salt and coarsely ground black pepper

2½ tablespoons olive oil

1 (14-inch) ciabatta loaf

1 large garlic clove, cut in half lengthwise

½ lemon

2 tablespoons coarsely chopped flat-leaf parsley

A couple handfuls of arugula

Just a little grated onion and garlic and a few select seasonings combine to make a stellar burger. Topped with whatever cheese I have on hand (usually blue for Joe, Cheddar for me), these are just the ticket for those nights when only a cheeseburger will do!

Speedy Weeknight Cheeseburgers

1⅓ pounds 85% lean ground beef

2 tablespoons grated onion

1 garlic clove, grated

1 tablespoon salt-free steak seasoning, such as Mrs. Dash

2 teaspoons Worcestershire sauce

½ teaspoon salt

4 hamburger buns, split

Safflower oil

3 tablespoons mayonnaise

1 tablespoon whole-grain mustard

4 slices of cheese, sized to just cover each burger

Sliced tomatoes, lettuce, and pickles

1 In a bowl, mix together the ground beef, onion, garlic, steak seasoning, Worcestershire sauce, and salt. Form into 4 patties, each about ¾ inch thick, pressing a small indentation into the center of one side of each patty to help hold the cheese.

2 Brush the cut sides of the buns lightly with oil and toast them, cut side down, in a cast-iron skillet over medium-high heat until golden brown.

3 Mix together the mayonnaise and mustard in a small bowl.

4 Set a 10-inch cast-iron skillet over medium-high heat. When it is hot, cook the burgers to your preferred doneness, about 3 minutes per side for medium-rare, beginning with the indented side down. When you flip them, indentation up, wait about 1 minute before topping each burger with cheese, allowing the cheese to melt as the burger finishes cooking.

5 To serve, smear some of the mayo-mustard spread over the bottom half of each bun. Top with a burger and the top bun. Pass the tomatoes, lettuce, and pickles at the table.

Need a recipe in your back pocket where just a few humble ingredients come together to taste like a million bucks? This Italian-style "mac and cheese" from my nonna—with its flavorful blend of pungent pecorino, mild parmigiano, and loads of black pepper—wins over hearts and taste buds every time. When I'm low on groceries, this is one dish I know I can put on the table, in a snap.

Spaghetti Cacio e Pepe

1 Bring a large pot of generously salted water to a boil. Add the pasta and cook for 2 minutes fewer than the package recommends. Drain the pasta, reserving about ½ cup of the starchy cooking water. Return the pasta and reserved cooking water to the pot.

2 Put the pot over medium heat and add the butter, both cheeses, and pepper. Cook for 3 minutes, stirring constantly to prevent sticking. Turn off the heat, cover, let stand for 1 minute, and then serve.

12 ounces dried spaghetti

4 tablespoons (½ stick) unsalted butter, softened

½ cup freshly grated pecorino cheese

½ cup freshly grated Parmigiano-Reggiano

1 teaspoon freshly ground black pepper

This dish is one of the standbys my mother made for us on days she was short on time or energy—or both. Trust me: We didn't mind one bit! I use good-quality deli ham in place of her prosciutto cotto, which can be hard to find, and I give it a tangy kick with Gorgonzola. I am quite certain she would approve of my updated version.

Bow-Tie Pasta with Peas, Ham & Gorgonzola

12 ounces dried bow-tie pasta

1 cup frozen peas

½ cup plus 2 tablespoons heavy cream

½ cup freshly grated Parmigiano-Reggiano

⅓ pound thin-sliced ham (6 to 8 slices), cut into ½-inch pieces

4 ounces crumbled Gorgonzola (½ cup)

Salt and freshly ground black pepper

1   Bring a large pot of generously salted water to a boil. Add the pasta and cook until it is al dente, following the package instructions, adding the peas about 30 seconds before the pasta is fully cooked. Drain and return the pasta and peas to the pot.

2   Put the pot over medium-high heat and add the cream, parmigiano, ham, Gorgonzola, and several grinds of pepper. Cook for 1 minute longer, season with salt and pepper to taste, and serve.

Because I tend to have all the ingredients on hand in my pantry, this is the dish I turn to when people stop by and I want to make something impressive but super easy. (Feel free to substitute whatever small pasta shape you like, such as penne or bow tie.) Slice a baguette, pour a glass of your favorite white wine, and you're all set with this one-dish supper.

Pasta Shells with No-Cook Tuna Sauce

1   Bring a large pot of generously salted water to a boil. Add the pasta and cook until it is al dente, following the package instructions. Drain well.

2   In a large serving bowl, toss together the tuna, arugula, tomatoes, olives, oil, parsley, and lemon juice. Add the pasta and toss to combine everything well. Let sit for 15 minutes to let the flavors mingle, or, to serve cold, refrigerate for up to 2 hours. Season with salt and pepper to taste, and serve.

8 ounces dried small pasta shells

2 (6-ounce) cans Italian tuna packed in olive oil, drained

2 cups arugula, coarsely chopped

1 cup grape tomatoes, halved, or quartered if large

¼ cup pitted Kalamata olives, chopped

¼ cup extra-virgin olive oil

2 tablespoons finely chopped flat-leaf parsley

Juice of 1 lemon

Salt and freshly ground black pepper

I love a traditional *puttanesca*—that spicy-pungent tomato sauce seasoned with garlic, capers, olives, anchovy, and crushed red pepper. But tradition doesn't keep me from putting my own spin on it when I'm in a rebel kind of mood. That's just what happened when one day it occurred to me that my nonna's much-loved grilled calamari salad was flavored similarly, with olives and capers. I slipped some grilled calamari into my *puttanesca* and loved the flavor and texture it added. Now, I make this version more often than the original!

Calamari Puttanesca

3 tablespoons olive oil

3 garlic cloves, sliced

4 anchovy fillets, packed in oil

Pinch of crushed red pepper flakes

1 (28-ounce) can crushed peeled Italian tomatoes

½ cup pitted Kalamata olives, cut in half

2 tablespoons capers, drained

1 pound calamari, cut into bite-size pieces

8 ounces dried spaghetti

Salt and freshly ground black pepper

2 tablespoons coarsely chopped flat-leaf parsley

1 Put a large (approximately 10-inch) skillet with high sides over medium heat. Add the oil, let heat for a minute, then add the garlic, anchovies, and red pepper flakes. Cook, stirring, until the anchovies "melt" and the garlic is lightly colored, about 1 minute.

2 Add the tomatoes, olives, and capers. Stir to combine, then simmer until thick and reduced, about 10 minutes. Add the calamari and cook over low heat until tender, 7 to 8 minutes.

3 While the sauce simmers, bring a large pot of generously salted water to a boil. Add the spaghetti and cook until it is al dente, following the package instructions. Drain.

4 Taste the sauce and season to taste with salt and pepper. Remove from the heat and add the parsley and spaghetti. Toss everything together to combine, and serve.

When I can't decide between a tomato sauce or a cream sauce, I combine the two. Since I like anything cheesy, the idea of this creamy Parmesan sauce coating perfectly cooked three-cheese tortellini seems almost too good to be true. Feel free to substitute a different pasta: the choice is yours.

Tortellini with Pink Parmesan Sauce

1   Put a large (approximately 10-inch) skillet with high sides over medium heat. Add the oil, heat for a minute, then add the onion, garlic, and a small pinch of salt. Cook until the onion has cooked down quite a bit, 5 to 7 minutes.

2   Add the wine and simmer to reduce by about half, then add the *passata*, sugar, oregano, dried basil, and granulated garlic. Simmer, covered, until the sauce has thickened and reduced, about 25 minutes.

3   About 10 minutes before the sauce has finished cooking, bring a large pot of generously salted water to a boil. Add the tortellini and cook until al dente, following the package instructions. Drain.

4   To finish the sauce, add the parmigiano, cream, and salt and pepper to taste. Cook for 1 minute longer, then add the drained tortellini and fresh basil, stirring to coat everything evenly. Serve immediately.

2 tablespoons olive oil

1 small onion, finely chopped

2 garlic cloves, minced

¼ cup dry white wine, such as pinot grigio

2 cups tomato *passata*, homemade (page 13) or store-bought

1 teaspoon sugar

½ teaspoon dried oregano

½ teaspoon dried basil

1 teaspoon granulated garlic

12 ounces dried three-cheese tortellini, such as Barilla brand

½ cup freshly grated Parmigiano-Reggiano

¼ cup heavy cream

Salt and freshly ground black pepper

6 fresh basil leaves, coarsely chopped

My traditional pasta alla Norma takes on a whole new attitude after adding sausage meatballs. A bit of the fat renders into the sauce, and the eggplant soaks it all up like a sponge. Ricotta salata is a form of ricotta that has been salted, pressed, and slightly aged into a semi-firm cheese that is perfect for shredding or crumbling.

Pasta alla Norma with Sausage Meatballs

1 small eggplant, cut into 1-inch cubes (about 2 cups)

Salt

½ pound mild Italian pork sausage with fennel, casings removed

¼ cup freshly grated Parmigiano-Reggiano

1 garlic clove, grated

1 tablespoon finely chopped flat-leaf parsley

4 tablespoons olive oil, or more if needed

1 small yellow onion, diced

2 cups tomato *passata*, homemade (page 13) or store-bought

8 ounces dried ziti or other medium pasta, such as penne or rigatoni

5 fresh basil leaves, torn

Freshly ground black pepper

3 ounces ricotta salata

1 Toss the eggplant with ½ teaspoon salt in a large colander. Top the eggplant with a small dish and put a large can on top of it, such as a 35-ounce can of tomatoes. Let stand for 15 minutes to press moisture from the eggplant.

2 To make the meatballs, mix the sausage, parmigiano, garlic, and parsley in a bowl until well combined. Use your hands to form the mixture into 12 walnut-size balls, setting them on a plate as you form them.

3 Put a large (approximately 10-inch) skillet with high sides over medium to medium-high heat. Add 2 tablespoons of the oil, then add the meatballs and cook until they are browned on all sides, 5 to 7 minutes total. Remove to a plate.

4 Return the pan to medium heat and add the remaining 2 tablespoons oil. Add the pressed eggplant and cook until it develops some color and cooks down somewhat, 5 to 7 minutes. Add the onion, along with a bit more oil if needed to prevent sticking. Cook until the onion begins to soften, 2 to 3 minutes.

5 Add the *passata* and the seared meatballs, including any juices that have collected on the plate. Reduce the heat to medium-low, cover the pan, and let simmer slowly for 25 minutes.

6 About 10 minutes before the sauce is done cooking, bring a large pot of generously salted water to a boil. Add the pasta and cook until it is al dente, following the package instructions. Drain, reserving ½ cup of the starchy cooking water.

7 Add the pasta and basil to the sauce. Add the reserved cooking water as needed, a little at a time, to make the mixture saucy but not runny. Season to taste with salt and pepper.

8 Crumble the ricotta salata over the top, and serve family style from the pot.

I sometimes make this dish the way my mother did, soaking dried chickpeas overnight in water with a bit of baking soda, then simmering them low and slow for hours until they take on a creamy texture. For this weeknight version, I use a sneaky little trick: I purée one can of chickpeas and add it along with a second can of whole chickpeas, to make a wonderfully creamy soup without all the time-consuming soaking and simmering. Please don't tell on me—my mother may never look at me the same way again.

Pasta with Chickpeas

1 Process one can of chickpeas in a food processor to make a rough paste.

2 Heat the oil in a large saucepan over medium heat. Add the garlic and red pepper flakes and cook for 1 minute. Add the puréed and whole chickpeas, parsley, rosemary, ½ teaspoon salt, and 4 cups of water. Bring the mixture to a boil, then reduce the heat and simmer for 15 minutes.

3 Add the pasta to the chickpeas. Season to taste with salt and the pepper. Cook until the pasta is nearly al dente, about 10 minutes longer, then cover and let stand for 10 minutes to let the flavors meld.

4 To serve, stir to combine everything well, then ladle into warm bowls.

2 (15-ounce) cans chickpeas, rinsed and drained

2 tablespoons olive oil

2 garlic cloves, minced

Pinch of crushed red pepper flakes

1 tablespoon chopped flat-leaf parsley

1 teaspoon chopped fresh rosemary

Salt

10 ounces (about 1½ cups) dried pasta, such as large shells

½ teaspoon freshly ground black pepper

If you have pancetta and eggs in your fridge or freezer, plus a little parmigiano, you've pretty much got what it takes to make this Italian favorite. The eggy-cheesy sauce coats the strands of spaghetti oh-so-perfectly, it's like dining on velvet. At our house, it serves four, or on a rough day, possibly two. We have even been known to have it for breakfast (it's bacon and eggs, after all!). Please don't judge us.

Spaghetti Carbonara

1 tablespoon olive oil

1 small yellow onion, finely chopped

4 ounces pancetta, cut into ¼-inch dice

¼ cup dry white wine, such as pinot grigio

1 pound dried spaghetti

4 large eggs

½ cup freshly grated Parmigiano-Reggiano, plus more for serving

2 tablespoons heavy cream

Salt and freshly ground black pepper

3 tablespoons coarsely chopped flat-leaf parsley

1 Heat the oil in a small skillet over medium heat. Add the onion and pancetta and cook until the onion is translucent, 5 to 6 minutes. Add the wine and simmer until it is reduced by about half, about 3 minutes. Set the skillet aside off the heat.

2 Bring a large pot of generously salted water to a boil. Add the spaghetti and cook until it is al dente, following the package instructions.

3 While the spaghetti cooks, in a small bowl, whisk together the eggs, parmigiano, cream, ¼ teaspoon salt, and plenty of black pepper.

4 Drain the spaghetti, reserving ¼ cup of the starchy pasta water. Return the spaghetti and reserved water to the pot. Add the egg mixture to the hot spaghetti, along with the onion-pancetta mixture and the parsley. Stir well off the heat for a full minute to fully and evenly coat the spaghetti.

5 Serve immediately, passing additional parmigiano at the table.

As I gathered up whatever vegetables were lingering in the fridge one day, I came up with this salad. What started out as one evening's catchall dinner has turned out to be one of my all-time favorites—light yet satisfying, with great texture.

Quinoa Salad with Poached Salmon

1 Poach the salmon: Put a wide, 3-quart saucepan with at least 3-inch sides over medium heat. Add the wine, garlic, lemon, dill, parsley, salt, a few grinds of pepper, and 2 cups water. Bring to a simmer, add the salmon, and cover the skillet. Reduce the heat to low and simmer gently until the salmon is opaque and flakes when gently pierced with a knife, about 12 minutes. Carefully transfer the salmon to a plate and let cool to room temperature.

2 Meanwhile, cook the quinoa: Put the quinoa in a strainer and rinse well under cool running water. Cook the quinoa, following the package instructions. Transfer the quinoa to a large bowl, fluff it with a fork, and let cool for 10 minutes.

3 Meanwhile, peel the cucumber and cut it into ½-inch dice. Cut the tomatoes into ½-inch dice, too.

4 Add the cucumber, tomatoes, parsley, mint, dill, and scallions to the quinoa. Drizzle the oil and lemon juice over the top and toss everything together well. Season to taste with salt and pepper.

5 To finish, flake the salmon into large pieces over the salad and gently toss to mix. Cover the salad with plastic wrap and refrigerate until cold, about 30 minutes, before serving.

SALMON

½ cup dry white wine

2 garlic cloves

2 lemon slices

2 sprigs fresh dill

Small handful of flat-leaf parsley leaves

½ teaspoon salt

Coarsely ground black pepper

1 pound skinless salmon fillet, pin bones removed

QUINOA

1½ cups quinoa

1 English cucumber

2 plum tomatoes

¼ cup finely chopped flat-leaf parsley

¼ cup finely chopped fresh mint

2 tablespoons finely chopped fresh dill

5 scallions, white and light green parts only, finely chopped

3 tablespoons extra-virgin olive oil

Juice of 1 lemon

Salt and freshly ground black pepper

When I crave risotto in the middle of the week, but don't have the time to stand by the stove, stirring constantly for up to half an hour, this recipe is my savior. This mock version delivers rich flavor and creamy consistency with considerably less effort. You might even fool an Italian with it.

Mock Risotto with Pesto & Turkey Marinara

2 tablespoons olive oil

1 pound ground turkey

1 small yellow onion, cut into ¼-inch dice

2 garlic cloves, minced

½ teaspoon salt

Freshly ground black pepper

1½ cups crushed tomatoes

1¼ cups long-grain rice

¼ cup basil pesto, homemade (page 15) or store-bought

¼ cup freshly grated Parmigiano-Reggiano, plus more for serving

1   Put a large (approximately 10-inch) skillet with high sides over medium heat. Add the olive oil and let it get hot. Add the ground turkey, breaking it up with a wooden spoon, and cook for 2 minutes. Add the onion, garlic, salt, and a good pinch of pepper. Cook until the onion has softened and the mixture begins to brown, about 5 minutes.

2   Add the tomatoes and 4 cups water. Bring the mixture to a boil over medium heat, then lower the heat, and simmer for 10 minutes.

3   Add the rice, cover, and cook over medium-low heat until just tender, 16 to 20 minutes, or as indicated on the package.

4   Stir in the pesto and parmigiano. Cover and let stand for 5 minutes before serving.

This simple dish of pasta and beans is one of my all-time favorite comfort foods and is the recipe-I often turn to at the end of a long and stressful day. To an Italian, pasta e fagioli without bread is a punishment; chunks of crusty Italian bread are a must for dipping into the flavorful sauce.

Pasta e Fagioli

1 tablespoon olive oil

2 ribs celery, cut into ¼-inch dice

2 garlic cloves

2 (14-ounce) cans small white beans, rinsed and drained

2 tablespoons tomato purée or tomato paste

10 ounces (about 1⅓ cups) dried ditalini pasta

A few fresh basil leaves

½ teaspoon salt

Freshly ground black pepper

1 Heat the oil in a large saucepan over medium heat. Add the celery and garlic. Cook just long enough to coat the vegetables in oil and get them started cooking, about 2 minutes. Add the beans and tomato purée. Stir in 5 cups water and bring to à boil. Reduce the heat and simmer for 30 minutes.

2 Add the pasta and cook until al dente, about 8 minutes, stirring occasionally as it cooks to prevent sticking. Stir in the basil and salt, and season with pepper to taste.

3 Cover the pan and remove from the heat. Let stand for 10 minutes before serving.

When deciding what to do with some leftover pesto and goat cheese in the fridge, I came up with this dish on a whim. The chicken is easy to prepare, and it makes its own sauce, which oozes out as you cut into the chicken. I call that a winner-winner chicken dinner!

Pesto & Goat Cheese–Stuffed Chicken Breasts

1 Preheat the oven to 350°F. Position a wire rack over a rimmed baking sheet.

2 To make the stuffing, in a small bowl, stir together the pesto, goat cheese, garlic, salt, and a few grinds of pepper.

3 To form the pockets to hold the filling, make a 1½-inch-deep slit down the thicker side of each chicken breast, running about three-quarters of the way down the length of the breast. Press the stuffing into the pockets.

4 Wrap each chicken breast tightly in 1½ slices prosciutto, making sure to cover the entire slit well. Seal the breasts shut using toothpicks.

5 Put a large (approximately 10-inch) skillet over medium-high heat. Add the oil, heat for a minute, then arrange the chicken breasts in the pan, top side down. Sear the breasts so that they are golden on both sides, about 5 minutes total.

6 Transfer the chicken to the prepared rack over the baking sheet, then put the whole thing into the oven and bake until the chicken is cooked through (170°F, using an instant-read thermometer, making sure you are in the chicken flesh—not the filling), 20 to 25 minutes.

7 To serve, transfer the chicken to plates, remove the toothpicks, and cut each breast into thick slices.

¼ cup basil pesto, homemade (page 15) or store-bought

4 ounces fresh goat cheese (about ½ cup)

2 garlic cloves, minced

½ teaspoon salt

Freshly ground black pepper

4 (6-ounce) skinless, boneless chicken breasts

6 slices prosciutto (about 4 ounces)

2 tablespoons olive oil

My nonna made many versions of sausage and lentils, all delicious. I'm building my own collection, too, and this recipe is one of my favorites. The sausage gives the sauce tons of flavor, which the lentils soak up to make a deeply satisfying dish. Black lentils are sometimes labeled Beluga lentils, because they look like caviar. If you can't find them, substitute brown lentils. I use canned ones in this recipe for convenience, but if you have a little more time, boil dried lentils in plenty of unsalted water until they are tender. You'll need about 2 cups dried for this recipe.

I serve this dish as my nonna does, accompanied by large chunks of crusty Italian bread, some fresh mozzarella, and red wine.

Sausages with Black Lentils

2 tablespoons olive oil

6 Italian chicken or turkey sausage links (about 1¼ pounds), cut in half crosswise

1 small yellow onion, finely chopped

½ cup dry white wine, such as pinot grigio

2 (14.5-ounce) cans black lentils, rinsed and drained

1½ cups low-sodium chicken broth

2 tablespoons tomato paste

½ teaspoon Italian seasoning, homemade (page 14) or store-bought

Salt and freshly ground black pepper

2 tablespoons finely chopped flat-leaf parsley

1 Put a large (approximately 10-inch) skillet with high sides over medium-high heat. Add the olive oil and let it get hot. Add the sausage and cook for 5 to 6 minutes, browning it on all sides. Add the onion and cook for 2 minutes, then add the wine and simmer to reduce it by about half, about 30 seconds.

2 Stir in the lentils, broth, tomato paste, and Italian seasoning. Bring to a boil, reduce the heat to medium-low, cover, and cook for 15 minutes. Season to taste with salt and pepper.

3 Serve family style, with the parsley sprinkled over the top.

Saltimbocca means "jumps in the mouth," the perfect way to describe the burst of flavor you will experience when you take your first bite. Usually made with chicken or veal, my version of this simple dish, made with buttery, white-fleshed halibut, is fancy enough to serve to friends or to treat my husband to something special. Wrapping the mild fish in salty prosciutto and searing it contributes wonderful flavor and a crispy exterior.

Halibut Saltimbocca

1 Lay 2 slices of prosciutto flat on your work surface, overlapping them so that they are the same width as a halibut fillet. Center a fillet over the prosciutto and lay 2 sage leaves over the top. Fold one end of the prosciutto up and over the halibut, tucking it under the opposite side of the fish. Fold the second side over, tucking it under the whole packet, enclosing the fish in a bundle. Repeat to make 4 bundles.

2 Put a large (approximately 10-inch) skillet over medium heat. Add the oil and butter and let them get hot. Add the prosciutto-fish bundles, seam side down, and cook until the fish is opaque and the prosciutto is crispy, 4 to 5 minutes on each side, depending on the thickness of the fish. Transfer the bundles to a plate and cover with foil to keep them warm.

3 Add the wine and parsley to the skillet. Simmer until the wine has reduced by about half and the sauce thickens slightly, about 2 minutes.

4 To serve, put a fish bundle on each plate and drizzle the sauce over the top. Serve with the lemon wedges.

8 thin slices prosciutto

4 (6-ounce) skinless halibut fillets

8 fresh sage leaves

1 tablespoon olive oil

1 tablespoon unsalted butter

⅓ cup dry white wine, such as pinot grigio

1 tablespoon finely chopped flat-leaf parsley

4 lemon wedges

The only bread crumbs you'll find in these meaty cakes are on the outside. Inside, mashed potatoes bind the cooked cod (or other flaky white fish) and lump crabmeat, keeping the cakes moist and letting the seafood flavor shine through.

If cooked cod isn't sold in your market, put the raw fish in a saucepan, cover with water, and add a few sprigs of parsley, a sprinkling of salt, and some peppercorns. Cook at a bare simmer over medium-low heat until the fish is cooked through and flakes easily when pierced with a knife. Remove the cod from the poaching liquid and let cool completely before using. For the potatoes, I like the texture and buttery flavor that Yukon Golds lend these, but I've also made them successfully with russets, so use whatever you have on hand.

Crispy Fish Cakes with Tartar Sauce

TARTAR SAUCE

½ cup mayonnaise

2 tablespoons Greek yogurt

2 tablespoons finely diced gherkins

2 tablespoons finely chopped fresh chives

1 tablespoon capers, drained and coarsely chopped

2 teaspoons whole-grain or Dijon-style mustard

Finely grated zest of ½ lemon

1 teaspoon fresh lemon juice

1 Mix the tartar sauce: Whisk together the mayonnaise, yogurt, gherkins, chives, capers, mustard, lemon zest, and lemon juice in a small bowl. Cover with plastic wrap and refrigerate for at least 30 minutes or overnight.

2 Start the fish cakes: Put the potato in a small saucepan, cover with water, and season with salt. Bring to a boil and cook until the potato is very tender when pierced with a knife, 20 to 25 minutes. Drain, transfer to a medium bowl, and mash well with a fork or potato masher.

3 Add the mayonnaise, mustard, lemon zest and juice, parsley, and chives to the potato and mix well. Add ½ teaspoon salt and a few grinds of pepper. Crumble in the crab and cod with your fingers so that they are in medium flakes. Stir to combine, then cover with plastic wrap and refrigerate for at least 30 minutes or for up to 2 hours.

4 Put the panko in a shallow bowl. Scoop the fish mixture into 6 mounds, using about ⅓ cup each and flattening them into ½-inch-thick disks with your hands. Transfer the cakes to the panko as you form them, turning to coat them on both sides.

5 Put a large (12-inch) skillet over medium to medium-high heat. Add ¼ inch of oil and heat for a minute. Put the fish cakes into the hot pan and cook until golden brown and crispy on both sides, about 4 minutes per side. Transfer the cakes to a paper towel–lined plate to drain briefly.

6 Put the fish cakes on plates and top each one with a dollop of tartar sauce; pass a bowl of the remaining sauce on the side.

FISH CAKES

1 medium potato, peeled (about 5 ounces)

2 tablespoons mayonnaise

1 teaspoon Dijon-style mustard

Finely grated zest of ½ lemon

1 teaspoon fresh lemon juice

2 tablespoons finely chopped flat-leaf parsley

2 tablespoons finely chopped fresh chives

Salt and freshly ground black pepper

8 ounces jumbo lump crabmeat

6 ounces cooked cod

1½ cups panko bread crumbs

Olive oil

When my husband, Joe, and I dine out at our favorite Italian restaurant, mussels are the first thing we order. When I make them at home, it's usually as an appetizer for family and friends. But served with a glass of pinot grigio and bruschetta for dipping into the richly flavored broth, these are easily a meal in themselves.

For the bruschetta, I use a *tostapane,* a simple metal contraption that quickly and evenly toasts bread slices to a beautiful golden brown over a gas stovetop. I brought mine back from Italy, but I have occasionally seen them in specialty stores in the United States. A grill pan will do the job quite nicely, as well.

White Wine Mussels with Garlicky Bruschetta

MUSSELS

2 pounds fresh mussels, beards removed

2 tablespoons olive oil

1 shallot, sliced thin

1 small fennel bulb, trimmed, halved, and sliced thin

⅛ teaspoon salt

Crushed red pepper flakes

3 garlic cloves, sliced thin

1 cup dry white wine, such as pinot grigio

BRUSCHETTA

8 to 12 slices Italian bread, each about ⅜ inch thick

1 garlic clove, cut in half lengthwise

Extra-virgin olive oil

2 tablespoons coarsely chopped flat-leaf parsley

1 Prepare the mussels: To remove the grit from the mussels, put them into a large bowl, cover with water, let soak for 10 minutes, and drain.

2 Heat the olive oil in a 6-quart stockpot over medium heat until it is hot. Add the shallot, fennel, and salt. Cook, stirring, until the vegetables are tender, about 5 minutes. Add a pinch of crushed red pepper flakes and the garlic and cook for 1 minute longer.

3 Add the wine and cook for another 2 minutes. Add the mussels, then cover the pot and simmer until they have opened, about 5 minutes. Discard any that do not open.

4 Meanwhile, prepare the bruschetta: Heat a *tostapane* or ridged grill pan over medium-high heat and grill the bread, turning, until grill marks form on both sides. Rub one side of each bread slice with the cut side of the garlic and lightly drizzle olive oil over the top.

5 Stir the parsley into the mussels, then tip them out into a wide, shallow serving bowl and serve surrounded by the bruschetta.

My grandfather was a fisherman, and one of my earliest food memories is of sitting on his lap when I was a little girl as he fed me clams with lemon juice—much to my nonna's disapproval. (She didn't think it a good idea for a child my age to eat as many raw clams as I did.) Clams and sausage are a match made in heaven; every time I serve this dish to guests, they tell me it's become their new favorite seafood dish.

If you cannot find canned cherry tomatoes, use peeled plum tomatoes, cutting them into ½-inch dice. (I find canned diced tomatoes to be too juicy for this recipe.)

Sausage & Clams with Tomatoes

1   To remove the grit from the clams, put them into a large bowl, cover with water, and let soak for 20 minutes. Drain and repeat.

2   While the clams soak, put a 6-quart stockpot over medium-high heat. Add the olive oil, wait a minute, then add the sausage, breaking it up with a wooden spoon. Cook, stirring occasionally, until it is fully cooked.

3   Add the garlic, cook for 30 seconds, then stir in the wine and tomato paste, allowing the liquid to simmer for about 20 seconds. Add the tomatoes, reduce the heat to medium-low, and simmer for 10 minutes longer.

4   When the clams are ready, lift them from the water in handfuls, shaking out as much water as you can, and add them to the pan. When they are all in, stir, then cover the pot. Raise the heat to medium and simmer, shaking the pot every few minutes to help the clams open and cook evenly, until all of the clams have opened, 7 to 15 minutes. Discard any that do not open.

5   Serve the clams and sausage and all their juices family style in a large bowl, or in individual bowls, sprinkling the parsley over the top.

4 dozen littleneck clams, scrubbed well

2 tablespoons olive oil

6 ounces spicy Italian sausage, casings removed

3 garlic cloves, peeled and sliced

½ cup dry white wine, such as pinot grigio

2 tablespoons tomato paste

1 (14-ounce) can peeled cherry tomatoes

3 tablespoons coarsely chopped flat-leaf parsley

Garlicky, vinegary chimichurri takes the leading role in this dish. In addition to flank steak, the bright, tangy sauce is great drizzled over so many things, like boiled potatoes for a different take on potato salad, or over grilled chicken or fish. I even use it as a salad dressing. It's wonderful to have on hand, and the perfect condiment if you are crazy about anything briny, citrusy, or vinegary, as I am.

Grilled Flank Steak with Chimichurri

1   Make the chimichurri: Process the parsley, onion, garlic, oregano, vinegar, salt, and a few grinds of pepper in a food processor or blender until everything is in small pieces. With the motor running, slowly drizzle in the olive oil until the mixture forms a sauce. Transfer to a bowl, cover with plastic wrap, and refrigerate for at least 1 hour, or for up to 2 days. (Let stand at room temperature for 30 minutes or so before serving.)

2   Season the steak: In a small bowl, stir together the paprika, chili powder, granulated garlic and onion, brown sugar, salt, and pepper flakes. Brush both sides of the steak with the oil and then sprinkle the spice mixture evenly over both sides. Set aside the steak on a plate for 10 minutes.

3   Heat a stovetop grill pan over medium to medium-high heat until it is hot. Grill the steak to your desired doneness, about 4 minutes on each side for medium. (For medium-well, add an extra minute or so on each side.)

4   Transfer the steak to a cutting board and cut it against the grain into thin slices. Arrange the slices on individual plates and drizzle some of the chimichurri over the top. Serve the remaining chimichurri in a bowl on the side.

CHIMICHURRI

1 cup flat-leaf parsley

¼ cup coarsely chopped white onion

3 small garlic cloves

3 tablespoons fresh oregano

3 tablespoons red wine vinegar

1 teaspoon salt

Freshly ground black pepper

⅓ cup extra-virgin olive oil

STEAK

1 tablespoon sweet paprika

2 teaspoons chili powder

2 teaspoons granulated garlic

2 teaspoons granulated onion

2 teaspoons (packed) light brown sugar

1 teaspoon salt

Pinch of crushed red pepper flakes

1 (16-ounce) flank steak

2 tablespoons olive oil

I rarely indulge in fried food, partially for health reasons, but also because I cringe at the thought of grease working its way into my clean kitchen. When I do allow myself the splurge, it has to be worth it. These melt-in-your-mouth chops justify both the calories *and* the effort. When I make them, I always picture my uncle Tony, who would linger by the stove, nab one, and devour it scalding hot, just as my nonna reached to take them from the skillet. They're that good, and since they cook up fast—you won't have to wait long, either.

Pork Chops alla Milanese

3 large eggs

1 large garlic clove, finely grated

2 tablespoons finely chopped flat-leaf parsley

½ cup plus 2 tablespoons freshly grated Parmigiano-Reggiano

Salt and freshly ground black pepper

1½ cups fresh bread crumbs

About 1 cup safflower oil

4 bone-in pork chops (about 1¼ pounds)

8 cups baby arugula

2½ tablespoons extra-virgin olive oil

1 tablespoon fresh lemon juice, or to taste

½ teaspoon coarse sea salt

Small block of Parmigiano-Reggiano

1   In a shallow soup bowl, whisk together the eggs, garlic, parsley, 2 tablespoons of the parmigiano, a good pinch of salt, and a few grinds of pepper.

2   In a separate shallow bowl, stir together the bread crumbs, remaining ½ cup parmigiano, a good pinch of salt, and a few grinds of pepper.

3   Put a 12-inch skillet with high sides over medium to medium-high heat. Add the safflower oil and let it get hot. (Put the handle end of a wooden spoon into the oil; if the oil bubbles vigorously around the handle, it's ready.)

4   Dip each pork chop into the egg mixture, then press bread crumbs onto both sides. Transfer the chops to the pan as you bread them. Cook until the chops are a deep golden brown on both sides, about 4 minutes per side, depending on their thickness.

5   As the chops fry, put the arugula into a large bowl and drizzle with the olive oil and lemon juice. Add the coarse salt and a few grinds of pepper. Toss to evenly coat the leaves. Use a vegetable peeler to shave parmigiano over the top.

6   To serve, put a pork chop on each plate and a mound of the arugula on top or beside it.

LEISURELY ENTRÉES

Clam & Corn Chowder

Slow-Simmered Split Pea Soup

Pasta Genovese

The Ultimate Italian Beef & Pastina Soup

Gorgeous Bolognese

Pasta al Forno with Vegetable Sugo

Tagliatelle with Mushroom Ragù

Spinach & Artichoke–Stuffed Shells

Meat & Three-Cheese Lasagne

Pasta with Braised Short Ribs

The Cheesiest Ever Broccoli Mac & Cheese Bake

Pizza Night: Classic Margherita & White Veggie

Paella

Cornbread Dumpling–Topped Chili

Rice & Bean Enchiladas

Biscuit-Topped Chicken & Root Vegetable Casserole

Eggplant Parm Bake

Nonna's Stuffed Peppers

Roasted Chicken Cacciatore

Herbes de Provence Roasted Chicken

Filet of Beef au Poivre

Pot Roast alla Pizzaiola

Mama's Italian Meat Loaf

Garlic-Stuffed Pork Loin

This easy soup doesn't require a lot of specialty ingredients, but two are critical. Living in southern New Jersey, I can get my hands on incredibly sweet, locally grown corn all summer long. And since the shore is less than half an hour away, I eat a fair amount of amazing seafood throughout the summer, including clams. These two ingredients—fresh corn and clams—are the key to a chowder that tastes like summer by the sea.

Clam & Corn Chowder

3 pounds littleneck clams, scrubbed well

3 slices thick-cut bacon, cut into ¼-inch dice

1 large onion, cut into ½-inch dice

2 ribs celery, cut into ½-inch dice

2 sprigs fresh thyme

1 tablespoon unsalted butter

2 tablespoons all-purpose flour

2 cups (½-inch) diced peeled russet or Yukon Gold potatoes

Kernels cut from 2 ears of corn (about 2 cups)

¾ cup heavy cream

½ teaspoon salt

Freshly ground black pepper

2 tablespoons coarsely chopped flat-leaf parsley

1   To remove the grit from the clams, put them into a large bowl, cover with water, and let soak for 20 minutes. Drain and repeat.

2   Meanwhile, bring a quart of generously salted water to a boil in a 6-quart stockpot. Add the clams, cover, and cook over medium heat until they all open, 7 to 15 minutes. Use a slotted spoon to transfer the clams to a bowl. Discard any that do not open.

3   Line a strainer with a couple of coffee filters to completely cover the surface. Set the strainer over a large bowl. Ladle the clam liquid through the filters to remove all of the sand. Set the strained liquid aside. Rinse the pot, and return it to the stove.

4   Pull the clams from their shells and chop them into bite-size pieces.

5   Put the pot over medium heat, add the bacon, and cook until it is crispy and has rendered its fat, 5 to 7 minutes. Transfer the bacon to a plate with a slotted spoon, leaving behind a couple of tablespoons of fat in the pot. (Discard any additional bacon fat.)

6   Add the onion, celery, and thyme to the pot and cook until they are translucent, 5 to 7 minutes. Add the butter and flour. Cook, stirring constantly, for 1 minute to cook off the raw flour taste.

7   Add the potatoes, corn, and 4 cups of the reserved clam liquid. Bring to a boil, then reduce the heat, and simmer, uncovered, until the potatoes are tender, about 30 minutes.

8 Add the cream, salt, a few grinds of pepper, parsley, and the reserved clams and bacon. Cook for 2 minutes longer.

9 Remove the pot from the heat and serve immediately, or cover and let stand for up to 20 minutes to thicken slightly before serving. Refrigerate leftovers in an airtight container for up to 3 days. To reheat, thin the chowder with a splash of cream or water.

This easy-peasy soup produces a richly flavored, hearty dish without ham hocks or having to soak the dried peas overnight. The secret is good-quality bacon, which contributes plenty of smoky-salty taste with a lot less effort. Once you try it, you'll understand how slow-simmering can develop intense flavor that rivals even more complicated versions, and that is so much better than opening a can.

Slow-Simmered Split Pea Soup

4 cups low-sodium chicken broth

1 cup split peas, rinsed and drained

1 tablespoon olive oil

3 slices bacon, cut into ¼-inch dice

1 small yellow onion, cut into ¼-inch dice

1 small russet or Yukon Gold potato, peeled and cut into ¼-inch dice

1 carrot, cut into ¼-inch dice

1 rib celery, cut into ¼-inch dice

½ teaspoon dried oregano

Salt and freshly ground black pepper

1   Put the broth, peas, and 4 cups water in a 3-quart stockpot. Simmer, uncovered, over medium heat until the peas are quite soft, about 50 minutes.

2   While the peas cook, put a medium (9-inch) skillet over medium heat and add the oil and bacon. When the bacon begins to render some fat, add the onion, potato, carrot, and celery. Cook until the vegetables soften and begin to take on some color, 4 to 5 minutes.

3   After the peas have softened, add the bacon mixture and the oregano. Reduce the heat to low and simmer until the potatoes are tender and the peas are creamy soft, about 30 minutes longer. Add salt and pepper to taste, and serve hot. Refrigerate leftovers in an airtight container for up to 5 days.

Many Italian sauces go by the name Genovese for the town of Genoa in northern Italy, but this is the one my *Napoletana* (southern Italian) mother often cooked for me when I was growing up. Since Genoa is so close to France, you might think of this dish as the Italian cousin to French onion soup.

Pasta Genovese

1 Put a 6-quart Dutch oven over medium-high heat. Add the oil, heat for 1 minute, then add the ground beef, breaking it up with a wooden spoon. Season with a generous pinch of salt and a few grinds of pepper. Cook until the beef is mostly cooked through and has begun to brown, 5 to 6 minutes.

2 Skim away most of the rendered fat, leaving behind about 4 tablespoons. Add the onions, carrots, celery, and another generous pinch of salt. Cook, stirring frequently, until the onions have cooked down quite a bit and begin to caramelize, about 12 minutes.

3 Add the wine, cook for 1 minute, and then add 2½ cups water. Bring the mixture to a boil, cover, reduce the heat to low, and simmer for 2 hours.

4 When the sauce is ready, bring a large pot of generously salted water to a boil. Add the pasta and cook for 2 minutes short of the package instructions. Drain the pasta and add it to the sauce, along with the parsley and parmigiano. Season to taste with salt and pepper.

5 Raise the heat to medium and cook, stirring constantly, for 2 minutes before serving.

3 tablespoons olive oil

1 pound 85% lean ground beef

Salt and freshly ground black pepper

2 pounds yellow onions (about 4 medium-large), cut in half, then into half-moons

2 carrots, cut into ¼-inch dice

1 rib celery, cut into ¼-inch dice

½ cup dry white wine, such as pinot grigio

12 ounces smooth (no ridges) ziti or penne

2 tablespoons coarsely chopped flat-leaf parsley

½ cup freshly grated Parmigiano-Reggiano

Bolognese, also called ragù, is one of two quintessentially Italian tomato-based sauces enriched with ground beef and pork. This northern style, ready in about an hour, is embellished with peas, carrots, and rosemary, and is classically served over pappardelle pasta, as I do, here.

To make the sauce ahead, prepare it through step 3, then let cool and refrigerate in an airtight container for up to four days. To serve, reheat the sauce while you cook the pasta, then continue with the remaining steps.

Gorgeous Bolognese

1 Put a Dutch oven over medium-high heat. Add the oil, heat for 1 minute, then add the ground meat, breaking it up with a wooden spoon. Cook until the meat is mostly cooked through and has begun to brown, 6 to 7 minutes.

2 Skim away all but 3 tablespoons of the fat. Add the onion and carrots to the pan and season with salt and pepper. Cook until the vegetables soften, about 5 minutes.

3 Add the wine and simmer to reduce by about half. Add the tomatoes and rosemary. Swish ¼ cup water around in the tomato can to catch any remaining bits, then add to the pot. Bring the sauce to a boil, partially cover the pot, reduce the heat to medium-low, and simmer for 1 hour.

4 When the sauce has about 20 minutes to go, bring a large pot of generously salted water to a boil. Add the pasta and cook until it is al dente, following the package instructions. Drain and return the pasta to the pasta pot.

5 Add the peas and season with salt and pepper. Increase the heat to medium-high and cook uncovered for 5 minutes.

6 Add half of the sauce and the basil to the pasta and toss to coat. Serve the pasta in shallow bowls. Spoon the remaining sauce over the pasta and grate parmigiano generously over the top.

3 tablespoons olive oil

1¼ pounds ground meat loaf mix (equal parts beef, pork, and veal)

1 yellow onion, cut into ¼-inch dice

2 carrots, cut into ¼-inch dice

Salt and freshly ground black pepper

¾ cup red wine, such as merlot

1 (32-ounce) can Italian crushed tomatoes

1 sprig fresh rosemary

1½ pounds fresh pappardelle pasta, or 1 pound dried

½ cup frozen peas

8 fresh basil leaves, coarsely chopped

Parmigiano-Reggiano

As I was growing up, my nonna's *pasta al forno*—a slow-cooked meat sauce and assembled with pasta, more meat, and cheese—was the highlight of the week. These days, I have quite a few vegetarian friends, so I worked out this equally satisfying meatless version.

To make ahead, refrigerate, wrapped tightly with aluminum foil, for up to three days. Let stand at room temperature for about thirty minutes before baking.

Pasta al Forno with Vegetable Sugo

4 medium portobello mushrooms

1 small yellow onion

1 carrot

1 rib celery

2 tablespoons olive oil, plus more for the pan

3 garlic cloves, minced

Salt

¼ cup dry white wine

32 ounces (4 cups) tomato *passata*, homemade (page 13) or store-bought

1 teaspoon Italian seasoning, homemade (page 14) or store-bought

Freshly ground black pepper

1 large zucchini, cut into ¼-inch dice

1 pound dried rigatoni

1 cup whole milk ricotta cheese

½ cup shredded Asiago cheese

1 cup freshly grated Parmigiano-Reggiano

6 fresh basil leaves, chopped

1 cup shredded mozzarella cheese

1   Snap off the stems from the mushrooms. Use a spoon to scrape away the gills from the underside of the caps. Discard the stems and gills or save for another use. Cut the mushrooms into ½-inch dice. Cut the onion, carrot, and celery into ¼-inch dice.

2   Put a large (approximately 10-inch) skillet with high sides over medium heat. Add the oil and let it get hot. Add the mushrooms, onion, carrot, celery, garlic, and ¼ teaspoon salt. Cook, stirring, until the vegetables have cooked down quite a bit and have developed some color, 7 to 10 minutes.

3   Add the wine, let cook for 20 seconds, then add the *passata* and Italian seasoning, and season with salt and pepper. Reduce the heat to medium-low and simmer for 20 minutes. Add the zucchini and simmer for 10 minutes longer.

4   While the zucchini cooks, bring a large pot of generously salted water to a boil. Preheat the oven to 400°F. Oil a 9 × 13-inch baking pan.

5   Add the pasta to the boiling water and cook it for 2 minutes fewer than the recommended time on the package instructions. Drain and return the pasta to the pot.

6 Add the sauce to the pasta. Stir in the ricotta, Asiago, ½ cup of the parmigiano, and the basil until everything is evenly mixed. Transfer the mixture to the prepared baking pan and top with the mozzarella and the remaining ½ cup parmigiano.

7 Bake until the sauce is bubbly and the top is golden brown, 20 to 25 minutes. Let stand for about 10 minutes before serving family style, straight from the pan.

A combination of earthy mushrooms lends great depth of flavor to this rich, luxurious sauce coating perfectly cooked strands of tagliatelle. Look no further for a vegetarian entrée worthy of a standing ovation!

Tagliatelle with Mushroom Ragù

1   Bring a large pot of generously salted water to a boil.

2   Meanwhile, bring 1 cup water to a boil in a small saucepan. Remove from the heat and add the dried porcini. Let steep for 10 minutes, then remove the porcini and cut them into small pieces. Reserve the soaking water separately.

3   Put a large (approximately 10-inch) skillet with high sides over medium heat. Add the butter and olive oil and let them get hot. Add the mixed mushrooms and cook, stirring occasionally, until they have reduced in volume, about 10 minutes. Add the onion, garlic, and ½ teaspoon salt, and cook until the onion softens, 6 to 7 minutes longer.

4   Add the wine and simmer to reduce by about half, then add the thyme, porcini, and the soaking water, holding back the last bit, which may be gritty. Add salt to taste and plenty of pepper. Simmer the sauce for another 10 minutes.

5   Meanwhile, add the tagliatelle to the salted boiling water and cook until it is al dente, following the package instructions. Drain, reserving ½ cup of the starchy cooking water.

6   Add the pasta to the sauce, along with the cream, tossing to coat the pasta. If the sauce seems thick, add some of the reserved pasta cooking water to make a velvety sauce that evenly coats the pasta. Add the parsley and parmigiano, toss everything together well, and serve immediately.

¼ cup dried porcini mushrooms

2 tablespoons (¼ stick) unsalted butter

1 tablespoon olive oil

1¼ pounds mixed mushrooms, such as shiitake, cremini, and oyster, stemmed and coarsely chopped

1 medium red onion, sliced thin

3 garlic cloves, minced

Salt and freshly ground black pepper

½ cup dry marsala wine

2 teaspoons dried thyme

8 ounces dried tagliatelle pasta

¼ cup heavy cream

2 tablespoons coarsely chopped flat-leaf parsley

¼ cup freshly grated Parmigiano-Reggiano

These decadent filled shells are bursting with four kinds of cheese, along with a good dose of vegetables to ease your conscience. I love the combination of spinach and artichoke, which explains my obsession with spinach-and-artichoke dip. Using frozen vegetables is a win-win: You get all of the flavor with no risk of pricking your fingers on artichoke tips, and, trust me, those tips are painful!

To make ahead, refrigerate, wrapped tightly with aluminum foil, for up to two days. Let stand at room temperature for about thirty minutes before baking.

Spinach & Artichoke–Stuffed Shells

FILLING

3 tablespoons olive oil

1 small yellow onion, finely chopped

3 garlic cloves, minced

1 (10-ounce) box frozen chopped spinach, thawed, drained, and squeezed dry

1 (10-ounce) box frozen artichoke hearts, thawed and coarsely chopped

¼ teaspoon salt

Freshly grated black pepper

1½ cups whole milk ricotta cheese

1 cup freshly grated Parmigiano-Reggiano

1 cup shredded provolone cheese

1 cup shredded mozzarella cheese

1 Make the filling: Put a large (approximately 10-inch) skillet over medium heat. Add the oil and let it get hot. Add the onion and garlic and cook, stirring frequently, until the onion is translucent, 4 to 5 minutes. Stir in the spinach. artichokes, salt, and a few grinds of pepper. Cook for 2 minutes longer. Set aside to cool completely.

2 Put the ricotta in a large bowl and stir in ½ cup each of the parmigiano, provolone, and mozzarella.

3 Make the sauce: In a large saucepan over medium heat, melt the butter. Add the flour and cook, stirring constantly, for 1 minute. Add the milk, whisking constantly. Add a touch of nutmeg, and salt and pepper to taste. Cook, stirring constantly, until the sauce has the consistency of heavy cream, about 4 minutes. Set aside to cool slightly.

4 Preheat the oven to 400°F. Butter a 9 × 13-inch baking pan.

5 Bring a large pot of generously salted water to a boil. Add the pasta and cook until it is al dente, following the package instructions. Rinse well under cold water to prevent further cooking, and drain.

6   To finish the filling, stir the cooled spinach mixture into the ricotta mixture until evenly combined.

7   To assemble, spread half of the sauce over the bottom of the prepared pan. Use a spoon to stuff the spinach mixture into the shells. As you stuff them, arrange the shells, seam side up, in the pan, packing them in tightly. Pour the remaining sauce evenly over the shells. Mix together the remaining ½ cup each of parmigiano, provolone, and mozzarella, and sprinkle evenly over the top.

8   Bake until the sauce is bubbly and the top is golden, about 30 minutes. Let cool for 10 minutes before dishing out 3 to 4 shells per serving.

SAUCE

5 tablespoons unsalted butter, plus more for the pan

⅓ cup all-purpose flour

3½ cups whole milk

Freshly grated nutmeg

Salt and freshly ground black pepper

12 ounces jumbo pasta shells (about 32 shells)

This is my favorite style of lasagne—the classic meat-and-cheese version I grew up eating. The slow-cooked sauce starts with sweet Italian sausage, and the cheeses are familiar ricotta, mozzarella, and parmigiano. Best of all, there's no need for fussy béchamel. You will find this dish on our table at every large family gathering, not only because it's easy on the cook and may be prepared in advance, but because everyone loves it. The recipe makes a little more meat sauce than you'll need for the lasagne, but you won't have any trouble using it. I freeze mine in an airtight container for up to two months, to have on hand for a quick pasta dinner.

To make ahead, refrigerate, wrapped tightly with aluminum foil, for up to three days. Let stand at room temperature for about thirty minutes before baking.

Meat & Three-Cheese Lasagne

1 Make the meat sauce: Put a 6-quart stockpot or Dutch oven over medium-high heat. Add the oil and let it get hot. Crumble the sausage into the pan and add the ground beef, breaking it up with a wooden spoon. Cook for 5 minutes. Add the onion and cook for 5 minutes longer. Remove and discard any excess fat in the pan, leaving about 4 tablespoons behind.

2 Add the wine and cook for 1 minute. Add the tomato purée. Partially cover the pan, reduce the heat to medium-low, and cook for 4 hours, stirring now and then.

3 Season the sauce to taste with salt and pepper. Stir in the basil leaves, roughly tearing them into pieces as you add them. Remove from the heat and let stand for 10 minutes.

MEAT SAUCE

3 tablespoons olive oil

1 pound sweet Italian sausage, casings removed

1 pound ground beef sirloin

1 medium onion, cut into ¼-inch dice

1 cup dry red wine, such as merlot

3 (28-ounce) cans tomato purée

Salt and freshly ground black pepper

½ cup fresh basil leaves

(recipe continues)

LASAGNE

1 pound dried lasagna

1 tablespoon olive oil

2 pounds whole milk ricotta cheese

1 cup freshly grated Parmigiano-Reggiano

1 large egg

Salt and freshly ground black pepper

12 ounces fresh mozzarella cheese, cut in thin slices

¼ cup coarsely chopped fresh basil leaves

4   Make the lasagne: Preheat the oven to 375°F. Oil a deep 9 × 13-inch baking dish.

5   Bring a large pot of generously salted water to a boil. Add the lasagna sheets and cook until they soften and are pliable, 4 to 5 minutes. They should not be fully cooked. Drain the pasta, rinsing with cold water to stop the cooking, and transfer to a large bowl. Toss with the oil to keep the pasta sheets from sticking together.

6   In a large bowl, stir together the ricotta, ½ cup of the parmigiano, the egg, a pinch of salt, and a few grinds of pepper.

7   Spread a thin layer of the meat sauce over the bottom of the prepared baking pan. To layer the lasagne, lay one-quarter of the lasagna (about 4 sheets) to fully cover the bottom of the pan in a single layer, with the sheets overlapping just slightly. Spread one-quarter of the ricotta mixture evenly over the noodles. Spread 1 cup of meat sauce evenly over that. Arrange one-quarter of the mozzarella slices over the top and sprinkle with one-quarter of the remaining parmigiano. Repeat the layering three times more, starting again with the lasagna sheets, to make four layers in all, ending with the mozzarella and parmigiano.

8   Bake the lasagne until it is bubbling enthusiastically and the top is golden brown, about 45 minutes. Carefully transfer the pan to a heatproof surface and let stand for 20 minutes. (The resting time helps prevent the lasagne from falling apart as you cut and serve it. It should stay hot for a good 40 minutes.)

9   Just before serving, sprinkle the chopped basil over the top. Cut the lasagne into generous squares, and serve.

10 Wrap leftovers in individual portions in foil and seal in a freezer bag. Freeze for up to one month. To reheat, thaw completely in the fridge, unwrap, and reheat in a baking dish in a 350°F oven until hot, 20 to 25 minutes.

I love walking through New York City's Little Italy, especially around the holidays: the lights, the sounds, the smells coming from the restaurants—they all feel like a taste of my southern Italian home. On one particular visit, we walked into the first place we found with an open table, and I ordered the pasta with braised short ribs. As I swooned over each bite of falling-apart meat, its rich, wine-infused sauce perfectly coating the pasta, I began to plot how I would re-create the dish in my own kitchen. Here is the result so that you can enjoy a piece of Little Italy—and the real Italia—in your own home, too.

The sauce and short ribs can be made ahead and refrigerated in an airtight container for up to two days. To serve, cook the sauce at a gentle simmer for twenty minutes, stir in the cooked pasta, and enjoy!

Pasta with Braised Short Ribs

1   Preheat the oven to 375°F.

2   Put a large Dutch oven over medium-high heat. Add the oil and let it get hot. Season both sides of the short ribs with ½ teaspoon salt and a few grinds of pepper. Dredge the ribs in the flour, shaking off the excess. Arrange the ribs in the pan and cook until golden brown and crispy, 3 to 4 minutes on each side. Remove the short ribs to a plate.

3   Add the carrots, onion, celery, and garlic to the pot, seasoning with ½ teaspoon salt and a few grinds of pepper. Cook, stirring frequently, until the vegetables soften, 5 to 6 minutes. Add the tomato paste and cook, stirring it into the vegetables for about 1 minute. Add the wine and simmer, stirring, until it reduces somewhat, about 1 minute. Add the rosemary, thyme, and broth, bring to a simmer, then return the short ribs to the pan, submerging them in the broth.

4   Cover and bake until the ribs are completely tender and falling off the bones, about 2½ hours, checking periodically and adding a bit of broth or water to keep the ribs submerged.

(recipe continues)

¼ cup safflower oil

4 beef short ribs (about 1½ pounds)

Salt and freshly ground black pepper

¼ cup all-purpose flour

2 large carrots, cut into ½-inch dice

1 large onion, cut into ½-inch dice

2 ribs celery, cut into ½-inch dice

4 garlic cloves, smashed and peeled

3 tablespoons tomato paste

1½ cups red wine, such as merlot

2 sprigs fresh rosemary

1 sprig fresh thyme

1½ cups low-sodium beef broth, plus more if needed

1 pound dried penne pasta

6 fresh basil leaves

Parmigiano-Reggiano

5 Carefully transfer the short ribs from the pan to a work surface. Use two forks to shred the beef into bite-size chunks, or let stand until cool enough to handle and shred the beef with your fingers.

6 Bring a large pot of generously salted water to a boil. Add the pasta and cook until it is al dente, following the package instructions. Drain well, reserving ½ cup of the starchy cooking water. Return the pasta to the pot and cover to keep it warm.

7 Skim any visible fat from the top of the sauce, then use an immersion blender to puree the sauce in the pot until it thickens slightly. (Alternatively, carefully transfer half of the hot sauce to a blender, process until smooth, then stir back into the remaining sauce.)

8 Return the shredded beef to the sauce and give it a good stir. Return the pot of meat and sauce to medium heat and stir in the pasta and basil, along with a little of the reserved pasta water, if needed, to keep it saucy.

9 Serve family style, with a generous grating of parmigiano over the top.

Those who know me might say that my love for any and every kind of baked pasta has reached the level of obsession. Stovetop mac and cheese is great, but I am compelled to take it to the next level, baked to gooey perfection and crowned with a crunchy topping. Dry mustard might sound like an unusual ingredient for mac and cheese, but trust me, it's the little secret that makes this dish outrageously good. I use corkscrew pasta because I love the way it holds the sauce, but feel free to use any small pasta shape of your choice. This dish is so popular among my friends and family that my best friend served it at her bridal shower. I ended up writing out the recipe by hand for nearly sixty women that day!

To make ahead, refrigerate, wrapped tightly with aluminum foil, for up to three days. Let stand at room temperature for about thirty minutes before baking.

The Cheesiest Ever Broccoli Mac & Cheese Bake

½ pound dried corkscrew pasta

2½ cups coarsely chopped broccoli florets

6 tablespoons (¾ stick) unsalted butter, plus more for the pan

¼ cup all-purpose flour

2 cups whole milk

1 tablespoon dry mustard

2 cups shredded extra-sharp Cheddar cheese

Salt and freshly ground black pepper

½ cup freshly grated Parmigiano-Reggiano, plus more for topping

¼ cup fresh or dried plain bread crumbs

1 Preheat the oven to 400°F. Butter an 8 × 12-inch baking dish.

2 Bring a large pot of generously salted water to a boil. Add the pasta and broccoli. Cook until the pasta is al dente, following the package instructions. Drain the pasta and broccoli and return to the pot.

3 Meanwhile, put a medium (3-quart) saucepan over medium heat. Add 4 tablespoons of the butter, wait for it to melt, then stir in the flour. Cook, stirring constantly, for 1 minute to cook off the raw flour taste. Pour in the milk in a slow stream while whisking constantly. Cook, stirring frequently, until the sauce has the consistency of heavy cream, 4 to 5 minutes. Add the mustard and Cheddar cheese, stirring in a figure eight motion, until most of the cheese has melted. Season to taste with salt and pepper.

4 Add the sauce and ½ cup parmigiano to the pasta, mixing to coat the pasta evenly. Transfer the mixture to the prepared baking pan.

5   In a small bowl, melt the remaining 2 tablespoons butter.
    Stir in the bread crumbs and then scatter the crumbs over
    the top of the pasta. Grate a bit more parmigiano over
    the top.

6   Bake until the sauce is bubbly and the top is golden brown
    and crispy, 20 to 25 minutes. Let cool for 20 minutes before
    serving.

Pizza holds a special place in my heart: My husband, Joe, and I met at a pizza shop, and the first thing I ever cooked for him was this white veggie pizza, which I formed into a heart. We even gave pizza cutters as our wedding favors! It's not just eating pizza I love, I adore *making* it—getting creative and using up veggies in the fridge. The classic Margherita takes me right back to the piazza in Napoli, while the white version remains Joe's favorite.

The pizza dough freezes well. Let it rise, wrap each piece in a resealable freezer bag, and freeze for up to two weeks. To use it, thaw completely in the fridge, then let it rest at room temperature for about thirty minutes before using it.

PIZZA NIGHT
Classic Margherita & White Veggie

1   Make the dough: Put the warm water in a bowl, stir in the yeast, and set aside until bubbly, about 3 minutes.

2   In the bowl of a standing mixer fitted with the dough hook, mix together the flour, salt, sugar, and oil. Stir in the dissolved yeast. Mix on medium speed until everything is combined, then reduce the speed to low and mix for 10 minutes.

3   Turn the dough out onto a work surface and divide in half, forming each piece into a ball. Put each dough ball into an oiled bowl large enough to allow it to double, turning the dough in the bowl to coat all of the surfaces with oil, then leaving it seam side down. Cover the bowls with plastic wrap and let the dough rise in a warm spot, such as inside a microwave oven, or in the oven with a pilot light on, until doubled in volume, 1 to 1½ hours.

4   When the dough is almost ready, put a pizza stone or baking steel in the oven and preheat to 475°F for at least 20 minutes. (If you don't have a stone or steel, form the pizza on an inverted rimless baking sheet following the instructions on page 94.)

(recipe continues)

PIZZA DOUGH

1⅓ cups warm water (110°F to 115°F)

1 (¼-ounce) packet active dry yeast

3½ cups all-purpose flour, plus more for shaping the dough

2 teaspoons salt

1 teaspoon sugar

2 tablespoons extra-virgin olive oil, plus more for the bowls

CLASSIC MARGHERITA SAUCE AND TOPPINGS

½ cup tomato sauce or tomato purée

Dried oregano

Dried basil

Granulated onion

Granulated garlic

Pinch of sugar

Salt and freshly ground black pepper

Semolina

8 ounces mozzarella cheese, shredded

A few fresh basil leaves

Olive oil

WHITE VEGGIE TOPPINGS

¼ cup olive oil

2 garlic cloves

1 (10-ounce) box frozen chopped spinach, thawed, drained, and squeezed dry

1 cup frozen cut broccoli, thawed and thoroughly drained

½ cup whole milk ricotta cheese

8 ounces mozzarella cheese, shredded

5   Make the Margherita sauce: Mix together the tomato sauce, oregano, basil, onion, garlic, sugar, salt, and pepper in a bowl. Add as much or as little of the herbs and flavorings as you like, starting with about ¼ teaspoon of each and adjusting to suit your taste.

6   To assemble the Margherita pizza, sprinkle some flour on a work surface. Remove one dough ball from its bowl and flour it lightly all over. Roll or stretch the dough into an 11-inch circle. Sprinkle semolina on a pizza peel or on the inverted baking sheet and put the dough round on top.

7   Use a ladle to put some of the sauce on the pizza, using the back of the ladle to swirl and spread the sauce to coat the surface of the dough, leaving a 1-inch rim without sauce all around. Arrange the cheese and basil on top of the sauce, and drizzle with olive oil.

8   Slide the pizza from the peel onto the stone by putting the front edge of the pizza peel onto the far end of the stone and shaking the peel to slide it off the stone. (Alternatively, put the inverted baking sheet topped with the pizza onto the oven rack.)

9   Bake until the crust is golden brown and the cheese is bubbly, 10 to 12 minutes, rotating the pizza halfway through the cooking time. Remove the pizza from the oven and top it with fresh basil leaves and a drizzle of olive oil.

10 Prepare the white veggie pizza: Put the oil in a bowl and grate the garlic over it with a fine grater; stir the garlic into the oil.

11 Sprinkle some flour on a work surface. Flour the second dough ball lightly all over. Roll or stretch the dough into an 11-inch circle. Sprinkle semolina on a pizza peel or on the inverted baking sheet and put the dough round on top.

12 Brush the garlic oil evenly over the surface of the dough. Distribute the spinach and broccoli over the dough, then use a

teaspoon to dollop the ricotta evenly around the top. Sprinkle salt lightly over everything, then top with the mozzarella.

13 Slide the pizza from the peel onto the stone by putting the front edge of the pizza peel onto the far end of the stone and shaking the peel to slide it off the stone. (Alternatively, put the inverted baking sheet topped with the pizza onto the oven rack.)

14 Bake until the crust is golden brown and the cheese is bubbly, 10 to 12 minutes, rotating the pizza halfway through the cooking time. Cut the pizzas into wedges, and serve hot.

This is the dish I turn to when I want to make an impression. It's magnificent to look at and boldly flavorful. The rice soaks up the salty-spicy flavors, then crisps at the bottom, my favorite part. Trust me: It's easier to prepare than you think. Bomba is the rice variety prized in Spain for paella. Italian Arborio rice also works, but may not absorb as much liquid.

Paella

1   To remove the grit from the clams and mussels, put them into a large bowl, cover with water, and let soak for 20 minutes. Drain and repeat a second time with the clams only.

2   Meanwhile, put a very large (18-inch) skillet or paella pan over medium-high heat. Add 2 tablespoons of the oil and let it get hot. Add the chicken, season with salt and pepper, and cook, turning frequently, to brown it on all sides, 4 to 5 minutes.

3   Move the chicken to one side of the pan and add the remaining 2 tablespoons oil to the center of the pan. Add the chorizo, onion, and garlic, and cook for about 5 minutes.

4   Add the rice and paprika, and cook, stirring, for 1 minute. Stir in the broth, tomatoes, and saffron. Bring the mixture to a boil, then reduce the heat to medium-low, cover, and simmer until the rice is al dente, about 15 minutes.

5   Arrange the mussels, clams, and shrimp over the rice. Cover and cook until all of the mussels and clams have opened and the shrimp is opaque, about 10 minutes. Discard any mussels and clams that do not open.

6   Season to taste with salt and pepper, then turn the heat to high and cook until the rice begins to brown on the bottom of the pan, 1 to 2 minutes. Scatter the parsley and lemon wedges on top, and serve family style.

12 Manila or littleneck clams, scrubbed and soaked

12 mussels, beards removed

4 tablespoons olive oil

1¼ pounds skinless, boneless chicken thighs, cut into 1-inch chunks

Salt and freshly ground black pepper

6 ounces Spanish-style chorizo, cut into ½-inch coins

1 large yellow onion, cut into ¼-inch dice

4 garlic cloves, minced

2¼ cups rice, preferably bomba variety

1 teaspoon sweet smoked paprika

6 cups low-sodium chicken broth

¾ cup canned diced tomatoes

Large pinch of saffron

1 pound large shrimp, shelled and deveined

½ cup coarsely chopped flat-leaf parsley

12 lemon wedges

I'm often asked by a friend to bring this when we gather at his home on a football Sunday. This dish is perfect for a crowd: It's easy, hearty, and satisfying. This recipe combines two of my favorite comfort dishes, chili and cornbread (in the irresistible form of dumplings), into a magnificent one-pot meal. Guacamole and sour cream are essential accompaniments.

The chili can be refrigerated in an airtight container for up to three days, or frozen in a resealable freezer bag for up to one month. To serve, bring the chili to a simmer in a large pot before making the dumplings.

Cornbread Dumpling–Topped Chili

CHILI

2 tablespoons safflower oil

1½ pounds 85% lean ground beef

1 yellow onion, cut in ½-inch dice

1 red bell pepper, cut in ½-inch dice

1 jalapeño pepper, seeded and minced

3 garlic cloves, minced

Salt and freshly ground black pepper

¾ cup lager-style beer

2 tablespoons chili powder

1½ tablespoons (packed) light brown sugar

2 teaspoons ground cumin

1 teaspoon dried oregano

2 tablespoons tomato paste

3 cups low-sodium beef broth

1 (15-ounce) can black beans, rinsed and drained

1 cup tomato purée

1 Start the chili: Put a 3-quart saucepan over medium-high heat. Add the oil and let it get hot. Add the ground beef, breaking it up with a wooden spoon, and cook until it is cooked through, about 5 minutes. Add the onion, bell pepper, jalapeño, and garlic, along with a good pinch of salt and a few grinds of pepper. Cook until the vegetables soften, 7 to 8 minutes.

2 Add the beer and simmer until it reduces slightly, about 30 seconds. Stir in the chili powder, brown sugar, cumin, oregano, another good pinch of salt, and the tomato paste until well mixed. Cook for 1 minute, then stir in the broth, beans, and tomato purée. Bring to a boil, then reduce the heat to medium-low, partially cover the pan, and cook until the mixture thickens quite a bit, about 2 hours.

3 When the chili is almost ready, make the dumplings: In a large bowl, whisk together the flour, cornmeal, chives, sugar, baking powder, and salt to evenly combine them. Stir in the milk and butter until just mixed.

4 Use an ice cream scoop or ¼ cup measure to scoop out 3-tablespoon dollops of the batter, transferring the mounds evenly over the surface of the chili. Cover and cook until the dumplings are puffed and cooked through, about 15 minutes, then remove the chili from the heat and let stand 5 minutes longer. Serve hot, family style.

DUMPLINGS

½ cup all-purpose flour

½ cup fine yellow cornmeal

2 tablespoons finely chopped fresh chives

1 tablespoon sugar

1½ teaspoons baking powder

½ teaspoon salt

½ cup whole milk

2 tablespoons unsalted butter, melted

I know you expect great Italian and Italian-American recipes from my kitchen, so what's up with the Mexican food? The truth is these two cuisines have a lot in common: red sauce, fresh and dried herbs, and peppers used to flavor starches (pasta, rice, tortillas) and legumes (chickpeas, black beans), often topped with cheese and served up family style to a hungry crowd. So this satisfying meatless entrée tastes a lot like home!

To make ahead, wrap tightly with aluminum foil and refrigerate for up to four days.

Rice & Bean Enchiladas

3 tablespoons safflower oil, plus more for the pan

1 small onion, cut in ½-inch dice

1 small red bell pepper, cut in ½-inch dice

2 teaspoons chili powder

1 teaspoon ground cumin

¼ teaspoon dried oregano

1 (4-ounce) can mild green chiles

1 (14-ounce) can black beans, rinsed and drained

1 cup cooked white rice

Salt and freshly ground black pepper

2 tablespoons coarsely chopped fresh cilantro

12 to 14 (6-inch) corn or flour tortillas

2 (14-ounce) cans red enchilada sauce

About 2½ cups shredded sharp Cheddar cheese

1   Preheat the oven to 375°F. Lightly oil a 9 × 13-inch baking pan.

2   To prepare the filling, put a large (approximately 10-inch) skillet with high sides over medium heat. Add the oil and let it get hot. Add the onion and bell pepper to the pan and cook until the onion is golden, 4 to 5 minutes. Add the chili powder, cumin, and oregano, and cook, stirring, for 30 seconds. Add the chiles, beans, and rice and cook 2 minutes longer. Add salt and pepper to taste. Transfer the filling to a bowl and stir in the cilantro. Set aside to cool slightly.

3   Briefly heat the tortillas until they are warm and pliable, one at a time, either in a small skillet or by waving them directly over a gas burner. Stack them on a small plate as you warm them.

4   To assemble the enchiladas, spread half of the enchilada sauce in the bottom of the prepared baking pan. Take a tortilla, smear a spoonful of sauce on one side, and top with some of the filling and some shredded cheese. Roll up the enchilada like a cigar and put it, seam side down, in the prepared baking pan. Repeat to fill the remaining tortillas and fill the pan.

5   Pour the remaining sauce evenly over the enchiladas and sprinkle the remaining cheese evenly over that. Bake until the sauce is bubbly and the tops are golden, 35 to 40 minutes. Serve hot.

This casserole of moist, tender chicken and vegetables in a creamy sauce topped with flaky biscuits is the ultimate chicken potpie. Rich and flavorful, it's perfect for a crowd on a cold winter's night, warming you up from the inside out. When rolling the biscuits, I cut the dough scraps into irregular pieces and bake them alongside the biscuits. When they emerge from the oven, I brush their tops with melted butter and sprinkle them with granulated garlic. Because, you know, I always have to have my cook's treat.

To make ahead, refrigerate, wrapped tightly with aluminum foil, for up to one day. Let stand at room temperature for about thirty minutes before baking.

Biscuit-Topped Chicken & Root Vegetable Casserole

1 Make the biscuits: In the bowl of a standing mixer fitted with the paddle attachment, mix together the flour, butter, sugar, baking powder, baking soda, and salt for just a few seconds to combine them evenly. With the mixer on medium, drizzle in the buttermilk, mixing just until the dough comes together in a ball around the paddle.

2 Gather the dough up into a ball and wrap it in plastic wrap. Refrigerate for 30 minutes or for up to 2 hours.

3 Roll out the dough on a lightly floured surface until it is ¾ inch thick. Use a biscuit cutter—any size or shape you like will do— to cut out the dough, cutting the biscuits as close together as possible.

4 Line a baking sheet with parchment and transfer the biscuits to the baking sheet, leaving an inch all around them. Cover with plastic wrap and refrigerate until you are ready for them, or for up to 2 hours.

BISCUITS

2 cups self-rising flour

5 tablespoons cold unsalted butter, cut into small pieces

1½ tablespoons sugar

1½ teaspoons baking powder

¼ teaspoon baking soda

½ teaspoon salt

1 cup buttermilk

1 large egg beaten with 1 tablespoon water

(recipe continues)

5 Prepare the chicken and vegetables: Put a 3-quart saucepan over medium-high heat. Add the oil, wait 1 minute, then add the chicken, sprinkling a good pinch of salt and a few grinds of pepper over it. Cook, stirring occasionally, for 5 minutes, then add the onion, carrots, celery, potatoes, and parsnips. Cook, stirring frequently, until the vegetables soften and begin to develop some color around the edges, 5 to 7 minutes.

6 Add the butter, stirring until it melts. Add the flour and cook for 1 minute, stirring continually to coat the chicken and vegetables and cook off the raw flour taste. Add the broth in a steady stream while stirring constantly, then add the thyme. Bring the liquid to a boil, reduce the heat to medium-low, and simmer for 15 minutes.

7 Add the cream, peas, and pearl onions, and cook for 10 minutes longer. Stir in the parsley. Season to taste with salt and pepper.

8 While the filling simmers, preheat the oven to 400°F. Oil a 9 × 13-inch baking dish.

9 Brush the biscuit tops with the egg wash and sprinkle them lightly with salt and pepper.

10 Pour the filling into the prepared pan and arrange the biscuits over the top. Bake until the sauce is bubbly and the biscuits are light golden all over, 20 to 25 minutes.

11 Serve family style, directly from the baking dish.

CHICKEN AND VEGETABLES

2 tablespoons olive oil, plus more for the pan

1½ pounds skinless, boneless chicken thigh meat, cut into 1-inch pieces

Salt and freshly ground black pepper

1 large onion, cut into ½-inch dice

2 large carrots, peeled and cut into ½-inch dice

2 ribs celery, cut into ½-inch dice

1 medium or 2 small potatoes, cut into ½-inch dice (about 1 cup)

1 large or 2 smaller parsnips, cut into ½-inch dice (about 1 cup)

4 tablespoons (½ stick) unsalted butter

¼ cup all-purpose flour

3 cups low-sodium chicken broth

1 tablespoon finely chopped fresh thyme

½ cup heavy cream

1 cup frozen peas, thawed

1 cup frozen pearl onions, thawed

1 tablespoon coarsely chopped flat-leaf parsley

When I was a child, my nonna would make a big pot of *sugo* on Sundays, then use it to prepare *pasta al forno* or gnocchi and eggplant parmigiana. These are staples in my home now, too, though this version of eggplant parm is slightly different from the classic one I grew up with. Layering cheese between the eggplant slices creates a seductively oozy-melty finish. I can't help stealing a few slices of fried eggplant as a snack while I'm cooking. A girl's gotta do what a girl's gotta do!

If your eggplants are large and you find them full of seeds when you cut them, you may want to add this extra step to reduce any possible bitterness: Lay out the eggplant slices on paper towels and salt them, then let them stand for one to two hours. Wipe the salt away with a paper towel before cooking them. With smaller, firmer eggplants, such as the Italian variety, you can skip this step.

To make ahead, refrigerate, wrapped tightly with aluminum foil, for up to two days. Let stand at room temperature for about thirty minutes before baking.

Eggplant Parm Bake

1 (32-ounce) can Italian peeled plum tomatoes

3 tablespoons olive oil

1 small yellow onion, finely chopped

Salt

3 garlic cloves, sliced or minced

Freshly ground black pepper

4 large eggs

1½ cups freshly grated Parmigiano-Reggiano

1 cup all-purpose flour

Safflower oil

2 medium eggplants, cut into ¼-inch-thick slices

6 fresh basil leaves

8 ounces fresh mozzarella cheese, sliced thin

1 Empty the tomatoes into a bowl and squeeze them with your hands to roughly crush them.

2 Put a 2-quart saucepan over medium heat. Add the olive oil, let it heat for 1 minute, then add the onion and ¼ teaspoon salt. Cook, stirring frequently, until the onion is translucent, 4 to 5 minutes. Add the garlic and cook for 1 minute longer.

3 Add the reserved tomatoes, a pinch of salt, and a few grinds of pepper. Bring to a boil, partially cover, reduce the heat to medium-low, and simmer for 20 minutes.

4 While the sauce simmers, prepare the eggplant. In a shallow bowl, whisk the eggs with ¼ cup of the parmigiano, ¼ teaspoon salt, and a few grinds of pepper. Put the flour in a shallow bowl or on a plate.

5   Put a Dutch oven or large (approximately 10-inch) skillet with at least 3-inch sides over medium to medium-high heat. Add ½ inch of safflower oil and let it get hot. (Put the handle end of a wooden spoon into the oil; if the oil bubbles vigorously around the handle, it's ready.)

6   Line a baking sheet with paper towels and put near the stove.

7   Dredge both sides of an eggplant slice in the flour, shaking off any excess, dip into the egg mixture, and add to the hot oil. Continue to coat and add eggplant slices until you have filled the pan in a single layer. Fry until the eggplant is golden brown on both sides, about 2½ minutes per side. Transfer the eggplant slices to the paper towels to drain as they are done. Continue to batter and fry the eggplant in batches until it has all been fried, adding oil between batches, as needed, and letting it get hot.

8   When the sauce is ready, tear the basil leaves into pieces and add them to the sauce. Season the sauce to taste with salt and pepper.

9   Preheat the oven to 425°F. Butter a 9-inch square baking dish.

10 To assemble the eggplant parm, spread 1 cup of the sauce in the bottom of the prepared baking dish. Arrange one-third of the eggplant slices in the pan to cover the bottom, overlapping them. Add about one-third of the remaining sauce, half of the mozzarella, and one-third of the remaining parmigiano. Repeat a second time, layering the eggplant, sauce, mozzarella, and parmigiano. Top with a final layer of eggplant, the remaining sauce, and the remaining parmigiano.

11 Bake until the sauce is bubbly and the top is golden, about 20 minutes. Let cool for 10 to 15 minutes before cutting and serving.

My nonna is a genius in the kitchen. Give her a sack of potatoes and she will turn it into something that will blow you away. One summer when we were visiting her in Napoli, she used leftover peppers to make us this dish. We all liked them so much (Joe ate two in one sitting!) that she and I now both make them weekly. The key lies in roasting the peppers, which infuses them with a smoky flavor that perfectly complements the rice and beef. Try them once, and I bet they will become a part of your weekly repertoire, too.

To make ahead, refrigerate, wrapped tightly with aluminum foil, for up to one day. Let stand at room temperature for about thirty minutes before baking.

Nonna's Stuffed Peppers

4 large bell peppers

8 medium plum tomatoes, cut into ½-inch dice (1½ cups)

½ cup white rice

1 pound 85% lean ground beef

1 large egg

1 cup (¼-inch) diced mozzarella or other cheese

¼ cup freshly grated Parmigiano-Reggiano

3 tablespoons finely chopped fresh basil

3 tablespoons finely chopped flat-leaf parsley

Salt and freshly ground black pepper

3 tablespoons olive oil, plus more for the pan

3 garlic cloves, minced

1 Roast the peppers over the flame of a gas burner, or broil them on a baking sheet, rotating them until the skins are blackened all over. Enclose the peppers in a paper bag, or put them into a bowl and cover with a plate, to allow the peppers to steam, which will make it easier to remove their skins.

2 When the peppers are cool enough to handle, hold one over a bowl to catch any juices and scrape away and discard the peel. Use a paring knife to cut an opening in the top and scrape out and discard the seeds, taking care not to break apart the pepper. Repeat with the remaining peppers.

3 Stir the tomatoes into the pepper juices in the bowl.

4 Cook the rice following the package instructions, stopping 10 minutes before the recommended cooking time. Drain and set aside.

5 Preheat the oven to 375°F. Oil a 9-inch square baking pan.

6 In a large bowl, mix together the ground beef, egg, mozzarella, parmigiano, basil, parsley, ¼ teaspoon salt, and several grinds of pepper. Stir in the rice and 1 cup of the tomato mixture until well mixed.

7 Stir 2 tablespoons of the olive oil and the garlic into the
remaining tomato mixture, along with ¼ teaspoon salt and a
few grinds of pepper. Spoon half of this tomato mixture into the
bottom the prepared baking pan.

8 Fill the roasted peppers with the meat mixture, packing it in
tightly but taking care not to break the peppers. Put the filled
peppers in the pan, laying them on their sides, and spoon the
remaining tomato mixture over them. Drizzle the remaining
1 tablespoon oil over the tops.

9 Bake until the peppers are golden brown on top, 60 to
65 minutes, and serve hot.

Every family has its own version of this Italian classic meant to satisfy the hunter's appetite after a hard day on the prowl. Mine is one of the easiest, but it does not sacrifice flavor: the spicy sauce simmers on the stovetop while the chicken roasts to perfection. Wait until just before serving to transfer the chicken thighs to the sauce, to preserve their crispy exterior. I can just about hear the crackle of that golden brown skin as I think about cutting into it.

Roasted Chicken Cacciatore

1   Preheat the oven to 400°F.

2   Put the chicken thighs in a roasting pan large enough to hold them in a single layer. Drizzle 2 tablespoons of the oil over the tops and sprinkle them with the Italian seasoning, ½ teaspoon salt, and a few grinds of pepper. Toss to evenly coat the thighs, then arrange them, skin side up, in the pan. Roast until the chicken is cooked through (internal temperature of 170°F) and the skin is deep golden, about 45 minutes.

3   Meanwhile, put a large (approximately 10-inch) skillet with high sides over medium-high heat. Add the remaining 3 tablespoons oil and let it get hot. Add the mushrooms, bell pepper, and onion and cook, stirring frequently, until the vegetables soften and develop some color, 5 to 7 minutes. Add the garlic and red pepper and cook for 1 minute more. Add the wine and simmer, stirring, until it reduces slightly, about 30 seconds.

4   Add the tomatoes to the skillet, along with the broth, rosemary, ½ teaspoon salt, and a few grinds of pepper. Partially cover the pot, reduce the heat to medium-low, and simmer for 30 minutes. Discard the rosemary stem.

5   To serve, spoon the sauce into a large, shallow platter. Nestle the chicken thighs into the sauce, skin side up. Tear the basil leaves into small pieces, sprinkle them over the top, and serve family style.

2½ pounds bone-in, skin-on chicken thighs

5 tablespoons olive oil

2 teaspoons Italian seasoning, homemade (page 14) or store-bought

Salt

Freshly ground black pepper

8 ounces cremini mushrooms, halved, or quartered if very large

1 red bell pepper, cut into ¼-inch strips

1 large yellow onion, cut in half, then into thin half-moons

3 garlic cloves, sliced thin

Pinch of crushed red pepper flakes

½ cup red wine, such as merlot

1 (32-ounce) can Italian crushed tomatoes

½ cup low-sodium beef broth

1 (3-inch) sprig fresh rosemary

6 fresh basil leaves

A good roasted chicken should be in every cook's repertoire. It makes an impressive entrée for a crowd, and a comforting cozy dinner for two (with leftovers!). This herb blend popular in the South of France ensures a flavorful result, while my technique will give you the crispy golden skin and tender meat you're after. This roasted chicken recipe truly rocks!

Herbes de Provence Roasted Chicken

4 tablespoons (½ stick) unsalted butter, softened

1½ tablespoons herbes de Provence

Salt and freshly ground black pepper

1 (5-pound) chicken, rinsed and patted dry

½ lemon

1 head of garlic, cut in half crosswise

2 (3-inch) sprigs fresh rosemary

3 (3-inch) sprigs fresh thyme

4 or 5 sprigs flat-leaf parsley

2 cups low-sodium chicken broth

1½ cups dry white wine, such as pinot grigio

1 Preheat the oven to 425°F.

2 In a small bowl, stir together the butter, herbes de Provence, ½ teaspoon salt, and a few grinds of black pepper.

3 Put a roasting rack in a roasting pan large enough to hold the chicken, and put the chicken on the rack. Stuff the lemon, garlic, rosemary, thyme, and parsley inside the cavity of the chicken. Tie the legs closed with kitchen twine. Loosen the skin on the top of the bird and rub half of the butter and herb mixture over the top of the chicken, sliding your hands beneath the skin to rub it evenly over the breast and thighs. Smooth the skin back into place, and smear the remaining butter mixture over the legs and thighs of the chicken. Season the chicken with salt and pepper.

4 Pour the broth and wine into the bottom of the roasting pan.

5 Roast the chicken until the internal temperature reaches 165°F in the thickest part of the thigh, 1 hour 15 minutes to 1 hour 25 minutes.

6 Transfer the chicken to a carving board that has a juice groove to catch the juices and let rest for 10 minutes. Carefully pour the pan juices into a fat separator, pouring off the fat (discard or save for another use) and retaining the juices.

7 Carve the chicken and pour some of the pan juices over each serving. Serve the remaining juices in a gravy pitcher on the side.

When I offer to make Joe a really special dinner, this is the one he asks for. Truth be told, it's a quick-fix dish—it takes all of about twenty minutes from start to finish, including making an easy pan sauce—but the fancy cut of meat and brandy make this a meal to be lingered over. Start the meal with a frisée salad topped with poached eggs (see page 219), and you'll feel like you're out for a fancy dinner at a bistro. Except that, if you're like me, you'll be ditching your heels for the fuzziest pair of slippers in your closet.

Filet of Beef au Poivre

1 Heat a 10-inch cast-iron skillet over medium heat until it's good and hot, 7 to 8 minutes. While the pan heats, season the steaks on both sides with the salt and plenty of freshly ground black pepper, pressing the pepper into both sides of the steaks. Let rest for 5 minutes.

2 Add the oil and 1 tablespoon of the butter to the skillet and give it a minute to get hot. Put the steaks into the pan and cook to your desired doneness, about 4 minutes on each side for medium rare. Transfer the steaks to a plate and cover with foil.

3 Add the shallots and the remaining 1 tablespoon butter to the pan. Cook, stirring frequently, until the shallots soften, 1 to 2 minutes.

4 Off the heat, add the brandy to the pan, scraping up any bits that have collected in the bottom of the pan with a wooden spatula. Return the pan to medium heat and simmer for 30 seconds.

5 Add the broth and let it come to a boil. Add the thyme and boil until the sauce reduces by about half, 2 to 3 minutes. Add the cream and cook until the sauce thickens enough to coat the back of a spoon, 1 to 2 minutes.

6 To serve, transfer the steaks to individual plates and spoon the sauce over them.

4 (4-ounce) filet mignon steaks, each a little more than 1 inch thick

½ teaspoon salt

Lots of coarsely ground black pepper

1 tablespoon safflower oil

2 tablespoons (¼ stick) unsalted butter

2 shallots, minced

3 tablespoons brandy

⅔ cup low-sodium beef broth

2 teaspoons fresh thyme leaves

2 tablespoons heavy cream

This is the pot roast of my childhood. The oregano gives it a distinctive flavor reminiscent of pizza, thus the name. My mother added cooked pasta and parmigiano to the mixture (shocking, I know), but I prefer to serve it over creamy polenta instead. The pot roast is also good stuffed into a ciabatta, topped with provolone, and baked until the cheese melts and the bread is crisp and golden.

Pot Roast alla Pizzaiola

2 tablespoons olive oil

2 pounds chuck roast, trimmed of any fat

Salt and freshly ground black pepper

8 ounces cremini mushrooms, halved, or quartered if large

6 garlic cloves, finely chopped

½ cup dry white wine, such as pinot grigio

1 (28-ounce) can Italian peeled plum tomatoes

¼ cup low-sodium beef broth

2 teaspoons dried oregano

6 fresh basil leaves, coarsely chopped

Roasted Garlic Polenta (page 145)

1   Heat a Dutch oven over medium-high heat. Add the oil and let it get hot. Add the roast to the pan and season it with ¾ teaspoon salt and a few grinds of pepper. Sear the meat for a few minutes on all sides to develop some color, about 8 minutes total, then transfer it to a plate.

2   Add the mushrooms and garlic to the pan, along with ¼ teaspoon salt and some pepper. Cook for 2 minutes, then add the wine and simmer to reduce for 30 seconds.

3   Empty the tomatoes into a bowl and squeeze them with your hands to roughly crush them. Add them to the pan with their juices along with the broth and oregano. Return the roast to the pan, along with any juices that have collected on the plate.

4   Bring the liquid to a boil, reduce the heat to low, cover, and simmer, stirring occasionally, until the meat is extremely tender, about 2½ hours.

5   Transfer the beef to a plate and shred the meat in large pieces with a fork. Return the shredded meat to the sauce and stir in the basil. Season to taste with salt and pepper.

6   Divide the polenta onto individual plates, spoon the pot roast and sauce generously over the top, and serve immediately.

7   Refrigerate leftovers in an airtight container for up to 3 days. To reheat, simmer gently until heated through, about 20 minutes.

My mother's meat loaf was often our Sunday *pranzo* (supper), filled with oozing cheese, salty salumi, and hard-boiled eggs, all wrapped in a crispy crust. Her Italian version is a bit different from the typical American meat loaf; it makes me hungry just to think of it.

Mama's Italian Meat Loaf

1 Preheat the oven to 350°F.

2 In a large bowl, mix together the ground beef, eggs, parsley, garlic, salt, and a few grinds of pepper. Stir in the parmigiano and bread crumbs, mixing well.

3 In a small bowl, combine the provolone, salami, and prosciutto.

4 Put a broiler pan on a rimmed baking sheet. Shape half of the meat mixture on the broiler pan into a roughly 12 × 5-inch loaf. Make an indentation running the length of the loaf, leaving about 1 inch at each end, and line up the whole cooked eggs along the center of it. Pack the provolone-salami mixture on top of and around the eggs. Press the remaining meat mixture over the filling to enclose the filling in the loaf.

5 Bake the meat loaf until browned on the outside, about 1 hour. Let cool for 10 minutes, then cut into slices to serve.

6 Refrigerate leftovers in an airtight container for up to 2 days. Reheat slices as my mother does: in a hot nonstick skillet coated with a light drizzle of oil for about 2 minutes on each side.

2 pounds 85% lean ground beef

2 large eggs

3 tablespoons finely chopped flat-leaf parsley

3 garlic cloves, minced

½ teaspoon salt

Freshly ground black pepper

1 cup freshly grated Parmigiano-Reggiano

⅓ cup fresh or dry bread crumbs

4 ounces provolone cheese, cut into ¼-inch dice

4 ounces mild salami or soppressata, cut into ¼-inch dice

4 ounces prosciutto, cut into ¼-inch dice

5 hard-boiled large eggs

Rosemary and garlic are natural partners to pork. This dish feeds a crowd using only a handful of ingredients. This is another dish that's great served over Roasted Garlic Polenta (page 145). In fact, when my friends know I'll be serving this pork loin, they insist on the polenta!

To prepare ahead, refrigerate the prepared but uncooked roast in its pan, tightly wrapped with aluminum foil, up to one day ahead. Let it stand at room temperature for thirty minutes before roasting.

Garlic-Stuffed Pork Loin

1 large yellow onion, unpeeled, cut into 6 thick rounds

2½ pounds pork loin

3 garlic cloves, cut into thin slivers

1 tablespoon fennel seeds

2 tablespoons olive oil

2 tablespoons fresh rosemary needles

Salt and freshly ground black pepper

¾ cup dry white wine, such as pinot grigio

1   Preheat the oven to 475°F.

2   Arrange the onion rounds, skin and all, in a single layer in the bottom of a 10-inch square roasting or baking pan. Cut slits all over the top and sides of the pork loin and stuff a sliver of garlic into each slit. Center the loin over the onion rounds in the pan.

3   Toast the fennel seeds in a dry skillet over medium heat until fragrant, 1 to 2 minutes. Let them cool for about 5 minutes, then pound the seeds with a mortar and pestle along with the oil, rosemary, 1 teaspoon salt, and a few grinds of pepper to make a coarse spice mixture. Smear the mixture all over the pork loin.

4   In a small bowl or measuring cup, stir together the wine, ¼ cup water, and a good pinch of salt. Pour this into the bottom of the baking pan.

5   Roast the pork for 15 minutes. Reduce the temperature to 400°F and continue to roast until the internal temperature of the pork reaches 150°F, 50 to 60 minutes.

6   Let the roast rest for 10 minutes before cutting it into thin slices. Serve with the winey pan juices drizzled over the top.

Panzanella Salad

Red Cabbage & Bacon Slaw

Spicy Black Beans

Kale, Mint & Radish Salad

Fennel & Orange Salad

Minty Pea Salad

Balsamic Roasted Beets

Parmesan-Roasted Potato Halves

Sautéed Garlic & Lemon Zucchini

Cannellini Beans with Pancetta & Spinach

SUPER-SIMPLE SALADS & SIDES

Cauliflower Stufato

Marsala Mushrooms

Shortcut Crispy Old Bay Fries

Wild Rice Pilaf

Cumin-Roasted Carrots

Creamy Buttery Noodles

Roasted Garlic Polenta

Cheesy Garlic Bread

As I was growing up, my nonna would make this salad to use up stale bread, which she softened with a bit of water in the traditional manner. I prefer making this salad with big chunks of crusty bread, which maintain their shape and texture even after soaking up the juices from the vegetables and dressing. The salad makes a substantial accompaniment, but I also enjoy it on its own, for lunch or as a light dinner.

Bocconcini are bite-size mozzarella balls. If you can't find them, use a good-quality, water-packed mozzarella, cut into one-inch cubes.

Panzanella Salad

4 cups cubed (1 inch) day-old bread, such as baguette

¼ cup extra-virgin olive oil

1 teaspoon Italian seasoning, homemade (page 14) or store-bought

1½ pounds beefsteak tomatoes, cut into large chunks

1 English cucumber, peeled and cut into ½-inch dice

8 ounces *bocconcini*

½ cup pitted Kalamata olives, halved

2 tablespoons capers, drained

1 garlic clove, minced

1 teaspoon sugar

1½ tablespoons red wine vinegar

¼ cup fresh basil leaves, torn into pieces

2 tablespoons coarsely chopped flat-leaf parsley

Salt and freshly ground black pepper

1 Preheat the oven to 400°F.

2 Toss the bread cubes with 2 tablespoons of the oil and the Italian seasoning. Spread out in a single layer on a baking sheet and bake until the bread is golden brown around the edges, about 10 minutes. Set aside until completely cool.

3 In a large bowl, combine the tomatoes, cucumber, *bocconcini*, olives, capers, garlic, and sugar. Drizzle the vinegar and the remaining 2 tablespoons oil over the salad and toss to evenly coat everything. Add the basil, parsley, and cooled bread, season with salt and pepper, and toss everything together well.

4 Before serving, cover the salad and let stand at room temperature for about 45 minutes, tossing it every 10 minutes or so, to allow the bread to soften and soak up the flavorful juices.

5 Refrigerate leftovers in an airtight container for up to one day, keeping in mind that the bread will become increasingly soggy as it sits.

This is the slaw my friends beg me to bring to summer barbecues. It's crunchy, of course, and creamy without being sloppy. But it's the bits of salty bacon, I think, that put this slaw over the top.

Red Cabbage & Bacon Slaw

¼ cup mayonnaise

2 tablespoons white wine vinegar

1 teaspoon Dijon-style mustard

1 teaspoon granulated garlic

1 teaspoon granulated onion

4 cups shredded red cabbage

2 tablespoons chopped scallions, white and light green parts only

5 slices bacon, cooked until crispy

Salt and freshly ground black pepper

In the bottom of a serving bowl, whisk together the mayonnaise, vinegar, mustard, garlic, and onion. Add the cabbage and scallions. Crumble in the bacon. Toss to coat the cabbage evenly with the dressing. Season to taste with salt and pepper, and toss once more before serving.

Despite my Italian heritage, I love eating and cooking Mexican food. When I'm cooking up a Mexican-style fiesta, black beans are a must for me. This smoky, spicy, saucy dish is just right alongside enchiladas, but I often let the beans take center stage, serving them in a bowl topped with avocado and salsa as an easy one-dish meal.

Spicy Black Beans

1   Put a 2-quart saucepan over medium heat. Add the oil and let it get hot. Add the onion, garlic, and jalapeño to the pan. Cook, stirring frequently, until the onion is soft and translucent, 5 to 6 minutes.

2   Add the beans, cumin, salt, and a few grinds of pepper. Stir to combine, then stir in ½ cup water. Cover and cook until hot and saucy, about 10 minutes.

3   To serve, top with a dollop of sour cream, if using, and sprinkle with the cilantro.

2 tablespoons olive oil

1 small onion, finely chopped

3 garlic cloves, finely chopped

1 jalapeño chile, seeded and minced

1 (32-ounce) can black beans, rinsed and drained

1 teaspoon ground cumin

½ teaspoon salt

Freshly ground black pepper

Sour cream (optional)

Coarsely chopped fresh cilantro leaves

While recently dining out in a New York restaurant, a kale salad dressed with chiles, mint, and lemon took my breath away with its simple, bold flavors. Seeking to re-create it at home, I substituted radishes (which I had on hand) for the peppery bite of chile peppers (which I did not). Radishes made a great salad even better, adding perfect punch and crunch, and they're prettier than chiles, too.

Kale, Mint & Radish Salad

Put the kale into a large bowl and add the radishes and mint. Drizzle the olive oil and lemon juice over the top, season with salt and pepper, and toss to coat the leaves evenly.

10 ounces baby kale leaves (about 8 cups)

5 radishes, very thinly sliced

¼ cup finely chopped fresh mint

3 tablespoons extra-virgin olive oil

Juice of ½ lemon, or to taste

Salt and freshly ground black pepper

I'm told I was given pieces of fennel to soothe teething pain as a child, so it should come as no surprise that I still love it. In Italy, we eat fennel as a palate cleanser between courses during big meals. My father insists on having cut fennel on the table when he comes for dinner. But in this recipe, fennel is the star, its anise flavor accenting juicy segments of sweet orange. It's a perfect example of the simple beauty that comes from combining just a few good ingredients. If they are available, use blood oranges in place of the navel ones for an even more gorgeous-looking salad.

Fennel & Orange Salad

2 navel oranges

6 cups mixed baby greens

1 (10-ounce) fennel bulb, trimmed, cored, and sliced very thin

1 tablespoon extra-virgin olive oil

½ teaspoon fresh lemon juice

Salt and freshly ground black pepper

1   Cut the tops and bottoms off of the oranges to expose the fruit. Stand each orange on one end and slice off all of the peel and white pith. Hold one of the oranges over a large bowl and use a paring knife to cut between each section and the membrane clinging to each side of it to release each section and drop the orange segment into the bowl. Repeat with the second orange. Squeeze any juice from the emptied membranes into the bowl; discard the membranes.

2   Add the greens and fennel to the bowl. Drizzle the oil and lemon juice over the salad and season to taste with salt and pepper. Toss well, and serve.

When most people think of peas, they think of something boring, flavorless, and probably overcooked, rolling around the food on the plate they *really* want to be eating. This simple recipe lets the peas take center stage, their sweetness balanced with bright vinegar and fresh mint that make this unassuming dish shine.

Minty Pea Salad

1 Bring a medium saucepan of salted water to a boil. Have ready a bowl of ice water. Add the peas to the boiling water and cook for 30 seconds. Drain the peas, then plunge them into the ice water to stop the cooking. Drain again and put the peas into a large bowl.

2 Add the oil, vinegar, and shallot to the peas, along with a small pinch of salt and a few grinds of pepper. Mix to coat the peas, then let stand for 15 minutes or for up to 2 hours.

3 Just before serving, add the endive, mint, and parsley. Toss well, season with salt and pepper to taste, and serve.

2 cups fresh or frozen peas

3 tablespoons extra-virgin olive oil

1½ tablespoons red wine vinegar

½ shallot, sliced thin

Salt and freshly ground black pepper

1 head Belgian endive, sliced very thin

¼ cup coarsely chopped fresh mint

2 tablespoons coarsely chopped flat-leaf parsley

In my opinion, people who don't like beets haven't had beets that have been cooked and seasoned correctly. Perfumed with balsamic vinegar, rosemary, and sweet red onion, and roasted until they are perfectly tender and caramelized, these beets are guaranteed to convert even the toughest critic.

Balsamic Roasted Beets

3 medium red beets, peeled (about ¾ pound)

1 small red onion, cut into large chunks

1 tablespoon fresh rosemary needles

1 teaspoon granulated garlic

Salt and freshly ground black pepper

2 tablespoons extra-virgin olive oil

2 tablespoons balsamic vinegar

1 tablespoon coarsely chopped flat-leaf parsley

1 Preheat the oven to 400°F.

2 Individually wrap the beets in foil, put them on a rimmed baking sheet, and roast until they are tender when pierced with a knife, about 1 hour. Let cool slightly and keep the oven on.

3 Unwrap the beets and cut each one into 6 wedges. Return the cut beets to the baking sheet, along with the onion, rosemary, garlic, a good pinch of salt, and several grinds of pepper. Drizzle the oil and balsamic vinegar over the vegetables and toss to evenly coat them.

4 Roast until the beets are completely tender, about 20 minutes longer.

5 Sprinkle parsley over the top, and serve.

In my own home as in my nonna's, a roast on the table always calls for roasted potatoes on the side. These are simple and simply delicious: parmesan gives the potatoes a cheesy crust, leaving the interior fluffy and tender. Leftovers? They're perfect for hash the following morning.

Parmesan-Roasted Potato Halves

1½ pounds Yukon Gold potatoes, halved lengthwise

2½ tablespoons olive oil

2 teaspoons Italian seasoning, homemade (page 14) or store-bought

½ teaspoon salt

Freshly ground black pepper

½ cup freshly grated Parmigiano-Reggiano

1 Preheat the oven to 400°F.

2 Arrange the potatoes in a baking pan large enough to hold them. Drizzle the oil over the potatoes and sprinkle them with the Italian seasoning, salt, and a few grinds of pepper. Toss everything together to evenly coat the potatoes, then turn them, cut side down, in the pan.

3 Roast the potatoes for 25 minutes, then flip them with a spatula and continue roasting until they are tender when pierced with a knife, about 20 minutes longer. Remove from the oven.

4 Set the oven to broil with a rack about 3½ inches from the broiler element.

5 Sprinkle the parmigiano evenly over the potatoes, then pop them under the broiler until the tops are golden brown, about 1 minute. Serve immediately.

When zucchini is at its peak of flavor throughout spring and summer, I use it in a million ways. Here, it develops a deep golden color from pan roasting, while the garlic adds bold flavor. The lemon and olive oil make a pan sauce that bathes each piece oh-so-perfectly. My nonna would often toss zucchini cooked this way with cooked pasta for a super-quick and easy dinner for my cousin and me.

Sautéed Garlic & Lemon Zucchini

1 Put a large (approximately 10-inch) skillet over medium-high heat. Add the oil and let it get hot. Add the zucchini and cook, stirring frequently, until it is golden all over, 9 to 10 minutes.

2 Reduce the heat to medium, add the garlic, and cook, stirring, for 2 minutes. Season to taste with salt and pepper.

3 Off the heat, stir in the lemon juice and parsley. Transfer to a platter, and serve.

2 tablespoons olive oil

1½ pounds zucchini, cut into 1-inch dice (about 3 medium zucchini)

2 garlic cloves, minced

Salt and freshly ground black pepper

1 teaspoon fresh lemon juice

1 tablespoon coarsely chopped flat-leaf parsley

I was rummaging through my pantry and fridge one evening, trying to come up with an accompaniment for the pork chops I was cooking. This dish fit the bill, with creamy beans, salty pancetta, and bright color from the spinach. A winning combination on the fly!

Cannellini Beans with Pancetta & Spinach

2 tablespoons olive oil

4 ounces pancetta or smoky bacon, cut into ½-inch dice

3 garlic cloves, minced

1 (28-ounce) can cannellini beans, rinsed and drained

6 cups baby spinach

¼ teaspoon salt

Freshly ground black pepper

1   Put a large (approximately 10-inch) skillet over medium heat. Add the oil and let it get hot. Add the pancetta and cook until crispy, about 5 minutes. Add the garlic and cook for 30 seconds longer. Add the beans and cook for another 2 minutes.

2   Add the spinach and salt, season lightly with pepper, and cook until the spinach wilts, about 2 minutes, adding a tablespoon or two of water, if needed, to help the spinach along. Serve immediately.

I grew up eating cauliflower, and this stewed (*stufato*) version was the method my mother turned to more than any other. The cauliflower becomes deliciously spicy and saucy, while retaining its shape and texture. This is my father's favorite way to enjoy cauliflower, and he beams with delight every time I make it for him.

Cauliflower Stufato

2 tablespoons olive oil

3 garlic cloves, sliced

1 shallot, sliced thin

Good pinch of crushed red pepper flakes

1½ tablespoons tomato paste

1 medium head cauliflower, cut into florets

2 tablespoons coarsely chopped flat-leaf parsley

Salt and freshly ground black pepper

1 Put a large (approximately 10-inch) skillet over medium heat. Add the oil and let it get hot. Add the garlic and shallot to the pan, and cook until they soften, 2 to 3 minutes. Add the pepper flakes and cook for a few seconds longer, then stir in the tomato paste.

2 Tumble in the cauliflower, stirring to coat the florets with the sauce. Add ½ cup water, cover, and simmer, stirring occasionally, until the cauliflower is just tender, 7 to 8 minutes.

3 Stir in the parsley and season to taste with salt and pepper. Transfer to a serving dish, and serve.

Mushrooms will soak up the flavor of just about anything you cook them in. One of my favorite baths for them is butter and marsala. Spooned over grilled steaks, or over Roasted Garlic Polenta (page 145), these can be—and often are in my home—a meal in themselves.

Marsala Mushrooms

1 Put a large (approximately 10-inch) skillet with high sides over medium-high heat. Add the oil and 1 tablespoon of the butter, and let them get hot. Add the mushrooms and cook until they cook down and begin to brown in spots, about 8 minutes.

2 Reduce the heat to medium, add the garlic and Italian seasoning, and cook 3 minutes longer. Raise the heat back to medium high, add the marsala, and simmer to reduce by about half, about 30 seconds.

3 Stir in the remaining ½ tablespoon butter and the parsley. Season to taste with salt and pepper, and serve immediately.

1½ tablespoons olive oil

1½ tablespoons unsalted butter

12 ounces cremini mushrooms, halved, or quartered if large

2 garlic cloves, minced

¾ teaspoon Italian seasoning, homemade (page 14) or store-bought

¼ cup dry marsala wine

2 tablespoons coarsely chopped flat-leaf parsley

Salt and freshly ground black pepper

I love me some French fries! I don't indulge in them often, so when I do, they've got to be good. This method produces the texture and flavor of traditional fries, but without the messy oil splatter. Old Bay gives them a spicy kick. Speedy Weeknight Cheeseburgers (page 30) and a pile of these fries equal my idea of heaven.

Shortcut Crispy Old Bay Fries

1   Put a nonstick baking sheet in the oven and preheat the oven to 425°F.

2   Prepare a large bowl of cold water. Use a sharp chef's knife to cut the potatoes into ¼-inch-thick slices, then stack the slices and cut into ¼-inch-thick strips, transferring them to the water as you cut them. Let stand for 5 minutes after you've finished, then drain the potatoes well. Lay out the potatoes on a clean kitchen towel and pat them dry.

3   Working in batches, put the potatoes in a single layer on a microwave-safe plate and microwave on high power until the potatoes have softened enough to become somewhat pliable, 3 to 4 minutes, depending on the wattage of your microwave. Pat the partially cooked potatoes dry with a kitchen towel or paper towels and transfer them to a large bowl.

4   Drizzle the oil over the potatoes and sprinkle with the Old Bay seasoning. Toss to evenly coat the potatoes.

5   Remove the baking sheet from the oven and carefully arrange the potatoes on it in a single layer. Roast the potatoes until they are crispy and golden all over, about 25 minutes, turning them with a spatula halfway through cooking.

6   Sprinkle the parsley over the potatoes, toss, and serve immediately.

3 large russet potatoes (about 1½ pounds), peeled

2½ tablespoons safflower oil

1 tablespoon Old Bay seasoning, or to taste

1½ tablespoons coarsely chopped flat-leaf parsley

I'm wild about wild rice! I just love its nutty flavor and chewy texture. Making this pilaf of mixed wild and long-grain rice is no more difficult than boiling ordinary rice, but its flavor is far from ordinary, with tons of herbs from the poultry seasoning infusing the broth.

This recipe assumes the wild rice needs forty-five minutes of cooking time and the long-grain rice twenty minutes. Check the package instructions on your wild and long-grain rice and adjust the timing, as needed, so that they will finish cooking at the same time.

Wild Rice Pilaf

1 tablespoon olive oil

1 tablespoon unsalted butter

1 shallot, minced

1 rib celery, diced

1 carrot, diced

6 ounces cremini mushrooms, coarsely chopped

½ teaspoon salt

¼ cup dry white wine, such as pinot grigio

1 cup wild rice

3 cups low-sodium chicken broth

1 teaspoon poultry seasoning

½ cup long-grain white rice

Salt and freshly ground black pepper

1 Put a 3-quart saucepan over medium heat. Add the oil and butter and let them get hot. Add the shallot, celery, carrot, mushrooms, and salt. Cook, stirring frequently, until the vegetables soften, 5 to 7 minutes.

2 Add the wine to the pan and simmer, stirring, until it has mostly evaporated. Add the wild rice, stirring to coat the grains with the vegetables. Add the broth and poultry seasoning. Bring the mixture to a boil, cover, reduce the heat to medium-low, and simmer for 25 minutes.

3 Stir in the white rice, cover, and cook until all the rice is tender, about 20 minutes longer.

4 Fluff the rice with a fork, add salt and pepper to taste, and serve.

Roasting gives vegetables deep, caramelized flavor and an appealing firm yet tender texture. Here, the technique intensifies the sweetness of the carrots, which is balanced by a savory note from the cumin seeds. This has become my favorite way to serve carrots because they provide great flavor and texture with such minimal effort. I often serve these alongside a roast, or chop and toss them with cooked quinoa and feta for a hearty vegetarian lunch.

Cumin-Roasted Carrots

1½ pounds carrots, each cut on a diagonal into 4 pieces

2 teaspoons cumin seeds

1½ teaspoons chili powder

1½ teaspoons granulated garlic

2 tablespoons olive oil

Salt and freshly ground black pepper

1   Preheat the oven to 425°F.

2   Spread out the carrots in a 9 × 13-inch metal baking sheet. Sprinkle them with the cumin seeds, chili powder, garlic, and olive oil. Add a small pinch of salt and a few grinds of pepper. Toss everything together to evenly coat the carrots.

3   Roast until the carrots are golden and crispy at the edges, 30 to 35 minutes, using a spatula to toss them halfway through. Transfer to a platter, and serve.

Perhaps you've seen the packets of noodles in powdered "sauce" at the supermarket. (Look closely and you'll see that many boast a "cheese-*flavored*" sauce, which may tell you something about their quality.) Maybe you've tried to save time by serving one as a side dish with dinner. Well, I walk right past them, because the garlicky-buttery goodness of this homemade version is beyond compare. It's just about as easy as the packet, too, so try it and you'll find yourself walking right by that supermarket aisle, too.

Creamy Buttery Noodles

1 Bring a large pot of generously salted water to a boil. Add the noodles and cook until al dente, following the package instructions. Drain, reserving ½ cup of the starchy cooking water.

2 Melt the butter in a 2-quart saucepan over medium heat. Add the garlic and cook, stirring, for 1 minute. Add the Italian seasoning and cook for a few seconds longer.

3 Pour in the reserved noodle cooking water, and simmer to reduce by about half. Add the cream and the cooked noodles. Cook for 1 minute.

4 Stir in the parmigiano and parsley, and serve.

8 ounces dried wide egg noodles

2 tablespoons (¼ stick) unsalted butter

3 garlic cloves, minced

2 teaspoons Italian seasoning, homemade (page 14) or store-bought

⅓ cup heavy cream

¼ cup freshly grated Parmigiano-Reggiano

1 tablespoon finely chopped flat-leaf parsley

Polenta is to most Italians what mashed potatoes are to most Americans: the ultimate comfort food. It was my first solid food and has remained a central part of my world ever since. I've never altered my nonna's recipe because, to me, it can't be beaten. It's simply the creamiest, most flavorful polenta I've ever eaten. The addition of sweet roasted garlic makes it unbeatable.

For a traditional Italian polenta, choose a medium to coarse cornmeal, such as Bob's Red Mill Polenta Corn Grits. For a finer-grained style, use a fine meal, such as Quaker Yellow Corn Meal. The polenta makes a great base for Pot Roast alla Pizzaiola (page 114) or Garlic-Stuffed Pork Loin (page 116).

Roasted Garlic Polenta

1   Preheat the oven to 375°F.

2   Cut the garlic in half crosswise and rub the oil over the cut sides. Wrap it in foil and bake for 45 minutes, until it is completely tender. Unwrap and set aside to cool.

3   Bring the cream and 2¾ cups water to a boil in a 3-quart saucepan or Dutch oven. Add the cornmeal in a slow, steady stream, whisking as you add it. Reduce the heat to medium-low, cover, and cook until creamy and no longer grainy, about 25 minutes, stirring every 5 minutes.

4   Add the roasted garlic during the last 5 minutes of cooking, squeezing the soft cloves from their papery shells into the polenta. Stir to incorporate the garlic.

5   Just before serving, stir in the butter, parmigiano, salt, and several grinds of black pepper. Serve hot.

1 head garlic

1 teaspoon olive oil

¼ cup heavy cream

½ cup stone-ground cornmeal, medium to coarse grind

2 tablespoons (¼ stick) unsalted butter

¼ cup freshly grated Parmigiano-Reggiano

1 teaspoon salt

Freshly ground black pepper

This winning garlic bread, which my dad created back when he owned his southern New Jersey pizza shop, remains one of my most treasured and requested recipes to this day. It has everything going for it: pungent garlic oil absorbed by bread that gets incredibly crispy in the oven, all topped with oozy cheese. It's absolutely irresistible.

Cheesy Garlic Bread

4 garlic cloves

2 tablespoons coarsely chopped flat-leaf parsley

¼ cup extra-virgin olive oil

1 loaf ciabatta or other Italian bread, cut in half horizontally

1 cup shredded mozzarella cheese

1 cup freshly grated Parmigiano-Reggiano

1 Preheat the oven to 400°F. Line a baking sheet with foil.

2 In a mini food processor or a blender, process the garlic, parsley, and oil to make a smooth pureé.

3 Smear the garlic mixture over the cut sides of the bread. Wrap the bread in foil, cut sides together like a sandwich. Bake for 10 minutes. Leave the oven on.

4 Unwrap the bread and open it so that the halves lie, cut side up, on the foil. Sprinkle the mozzarella and parmigiano evenly over the surface. Slide a baking sheet under the foil and bake, uncovered, until the cheese is golden brown and bubbly, 10 to 15 minutes.

5 Cut into slices, and serve immediately.

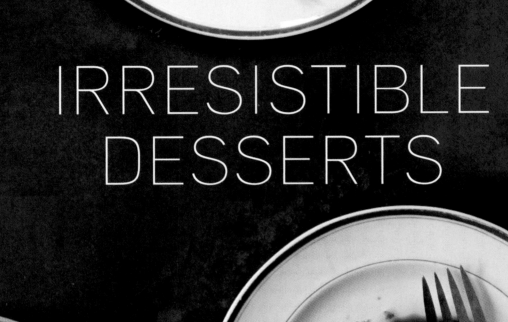

IRRESISTIBLE DESSERTS

Jammy Crème Brûlée

Cherry-Chocolate Puddings

Orange–Vanilla Bean Bread Pudding

Pomegranate Eton Mess

Citrus Meringue Pie

Toffee Apple Crumble

Yellow Cake with Raspberry Jam
& Orange Whipped Cream

Churros with Chocolate Dipping Sauce

Hazelnut Tiramisù

Caramel & Chocolate
Shortbread Tart

No-Bake Nutella Cheesecake

Devilishly Good Devil's Food Cake

Stunning Pavlova

Red Velvet Cupcakes

Mama's Babà al Rum

Peach Melba

Most people are intimidated by the thought of making crème brûlée, the classic French custard hidden under a shattering caramelized sugar shell. I'm not sure why—it's easy to make. Invest in a small kitchen torch and delight your guests with some crème brûlée drama whenever your heart desires. I tuck a small spoonful of jam in the bottom of my ramekin for a surprise burst of sticky sweetness. Choose a jam with whole berries, or the preserves of your choice.

    This dessert takes some advance planning. Once baked and cooled, it needs at least three hours in the fridge. Make the custards the night before and you'll have dessert all ready to go—just top with sugar and caramelize before serving.

Jammy Crème Brûlée

1¾ cups heavy cream

4 large egg yolks

1 teaspoon vanilla bean paste, or seeds scraped from 1 vanilla bean

½ cup sugar

1 teaspoon grated orange zest

⅛ teaspoon salt

4 teaspoons blackberry jam

1 Preheat the oven to 300°F.

2 In a small saucepan over low heat, heat the cream to simmering; do not boil. Remove from the heat.

3 In a bowl, using a stand mixer at medium speed, mix together the egg yolks, vanilla, and ¼ cup of the sugar until thick and pale, about 3 minutes. With the mixer on low, add the warm cream in a slow stream. Add the orange zest and salt, mixing just to combine. Spoon off and discard any foam from the surface.

4 Put 1 teaspoon of jam in the bottom of each of 4 (6-ounce) ramekins and put the ramekins into a roasting pan. Pour the custard over the jam to fill them equally.

5 Bring a kettle of water to a boil. Set the pan with the custards onto the oven rack and carefully pour in the water so that it comes halfway up the sides of the ramekins.

6 Bake the custards until they are softly set around the edges but still jiggle a bit in the center when you gently (and carefully!) jostle the pan, about 45 minutes.

7   Carefully remove the custards from the pan and let them cool at room temperature, at least 30 minutes. Cover with plastic wrap and refrigerate for at least 3 hours or overnight.

8   To serve, let the custards stand at room temperature for 10 minutes. Sprinkle 1 tablespoon of the remaining sugar evenly over the top of each. Wave a kitchen torch over the top of each custard to evenly melt and caramelize the sugar. Alternatively, put an oven rack in the top third of the oven, turn the oven to Broil, and put the ramekins on a baking sheet. Put the baking sheet under the broiler until the sugar is golden brown and bubbly, about 20 seconds, keeping a close eye on them, as they can quickly go from brown to burnt.

9   Wait a minute for the sugar to cool and harden, and serve.

In my teen years, I was obsessed with chocolate-covered cherries. While making chocolate pudding recently, I was overwhelmed with a desire to add a sweet cherry compote to this simple dessert. Truth be told, I still find the combination quite exciting.

Cherry-Chocolate Puddings

CHERRY COMPOTE

2 cups pitted fresh or thawed, frozen sweet cherries

¼ cup sugar

Juice of ½ lemon

1 tablespoon cornstarch

2 tablespoons cherry brandy (optional)

CUSTARD

6 ounces semisweet chocolate chips

1 cup heavy cream

½ cup whole milk

2 large eggs

¼ cup vanilla sugar, or ¼ cup sugar plus ¼ teaspoon pure vanilla extract

¼ teaspoon salt

1 teaspoon pure vanilla extract

1   Make the cherry compote: Put a 2-quart saucepan over medium heat. Add the cherries, sugar, and lemon juice and cook until the cherries begin to soften and release their juices, about 7 minutes.

2   In a small bowl, mix together the cornstarch with 1 tablespoon water. Add it to the cherry mixture along with the brandy, if using. Boil until thickened, about 1 minute. Transfer to a bowl and refrigerate until completely cool.

3   Make the custard: Put the chocolate in a bowl and set a fine-mesh strainer over it. In a small saucepan, bring the cream and milk to a simmer. In a medium bowl, whisk the eggs and vanilla sugar until pale and slightly thickened, about 3 minutes.

4   Add about half of the cream mixture to the egg mixture in a slow stream, whisking constantly. Whisk all of the egg-cream mixture back into the pan. Whisk in the salt. Cook over low heat, stirring constantly, until thick enough to coat the back of a wooden spoon, 10 to 12 minutes.

5   Stir in the vanilla and remove from the heat. Pour the custard into the strainer over the chocolate. Let stand for 3 minutes before stirring gently until smooth.

6   Divide the cherry compote among 6 (6-ounce) serving bowls. Spoon the custard over the compote. Cover the bowls with plastic wrap, pressing the wrap directly onto the surface of the custard. Refrigerate until cold and set, at least 3 hours or overnight.

If you're Italian, chances are every Christmas you receive a panettone from each of your aunts and uncles. By the end of the holiday, there's a lineup of these delicious, moist, eggy, citrus-scented fruit cakes on your kitchen counter. One year, I used some of my leftover panettone to make one of the best bread puddings ever. But then I had a problem: I didn't want to wait for panettone season to roll around to have it again. So I created this recipe, with plenty of orange zest and vanilla, to mimic that lovely flavor year-round.

Orange–Vanilla Bean Bread Pudding

1 In a large bowl, whisk together the eggs, milk, cream, granulated and brown sugars, orange zest, vanilla, and salt.

2 Butter an 8 × 12-inch baking dish. Scatter the bread cubes evenly into the prepared baking dish and pour the custard evenly over them. Use a spatula to press down on the bread to help it soak up some of the custard. Cover with foil and refrigerate for at least 2 hours or up to 8 hours.

3 Preheat the oven to 350°F.

4 Bake the pudding, covered, for 30 minutes. Remove the foil and return the pudding to the oven until the top is golden and the center is set or only slightly jiggly, 30 to 40 minutes longer.

5 Let cool for at least 20 minutes before serving warm or at room temperature.

6 large eggs

2 cups milk

1 cup heavy cream

½ cup granulated sugar

¼ cup (packed) light brown sugar

Finely grated zest of 1 orange

2 teaspoons vanilla bean paste or pure vanilla extract

¼ teaspoon salt

Butter, for pan

1 pound challah or brioche, cut into 1-inch cubes

I created this twist on the traditional English dessert one night to serve to a crowd of twelve. People go crazy for this mash-up of meringue, cream, and fruit. Yet, it's easy to make—especially if you purchase the meringues, as I do—and it also can easily be doubled or more to serve a crowd. Serve in glass dishes that showcase the ruby-red pomegranate seeds running through the winter-white cream.

Pomegranate Eton Mess

1½ cups pomegranate seeds

3 tablespoons pomegranate juice

1 tablespoon granulated sugar

1¼ cups heavy cream

¼ cup confectioners' sugar

8 (2-inch) meringues

1   In a small bowl, mix together the pomegranate seeds, juice, and granulated sugar. Set aside.

2   Using a chilled bowl and beaters, whip the cream with the confectioners' sugar until semi-stiff peaks form. Crumble the meringues into the whipped cream and stir, then briefly fold in the pomegranate mixture, leaving plenty of streaks. Spoon into 6 bowls or glasses, and serve.

Over the years, I have been dubbed the Citrus Queen, a tribute to my obsession with these puckery sweet-tart fruits. I love citrus for the way it makes most anything come to life, including this favorite pie. Traditionally, this pie is made with lemon, but why limit yourself to just one kind of fruit when you can double the flavor by using two?

Citrus Meringue Pie

1   Make the crust: Briefly pulse the flour and salt in a food processor. Add the butter and shortening and pulse until they are the size of peas. With the motor running, drizzle in the ice water, a tablespoon at a time, until the dough holds together when you pinch it between your fingers. (The crust can also be prepared in a stand mixer fitted with the paddle attachment.)

2   Turn the dough out onto a lightly floured work surface and, without handling it more than necessary, press into a flat disk. Wrap the dough in plastic wrap and refrigerate for at least 30 minutes or overnight.

3   Preheat the oven to 375°F. Spray a 9-inch pie pan with nonstick pan spray.

4   Roll out the crust on a floured surface into a 12-inch round. Transfer the crust to the prepared pan and settle it into the bottom and sides of the pan. Use a fork to prick the bottom and sides all over. Trim away any overhang and crimp the edges.

5   Line the crust with foil, shiny side down, and fill with dried beans or rice to prevent the crust from puffing or shrinking. Bake for 15 minutes.

(recipe continues)

CRUST

1½ cups all-purpose flour, plus more for rolling

¼ teaspoon salt

5 tablespoons cold unsalted butter, cut into small pieces

4 tablespoons cold vegetable shortening, cut into small pieces

Up to 3 tablespoons ice water

Nonstick cooking spray

MERINGUE

4 large egg whites, at room temperature

¼ teaspoon cream of tartar

6 tablespoons superfine sugar

FILLING

1 cup granulated sugar

¼ cup cornstarch

¼ teaspoon salt

Finely grated zest and juice of 1 large lemon

Finely grated zest and juice of 1 orange

2 tablespoons (¼ stick) unsalted butter

4 large egg yolks, beaten

6   Meanwhile, make the meringue topping: In a bowl of a stand mixer, beat the egg whites and cream of tartar until frothy. Add the superfine sugar, 1 tablespoon at a time, whisking after each addition to incorporate the sugar. Continue to whip until stiff peaks form.

7   After the crust has baked for 15 minutes, remove the foil and beans, then bake until light golden, 12 to 14 minutes longer. Remove the crust from the oven and leave the oven on.

8   Meanwhile, make the filling: In a 2-quart saucepan off the heat, whisk together the sugar, cornstarch, salt, the lemon and orange zests and juices, and 1½ cups water. Bring the mixture to a gentle boil over medium heat, whisking constantly to avoid forming lumps. Add the butter, whisking until it melts.

9   Put the yolks in a small bowl and drizzle in ½ cup of the hot citrus syrup in a slow, steady stream, whisking constantly. Whisk this mixture back into the pan and cook, whisking constantly, for 1 minute longer, taking care not to let the mixture boil.

10 Pour the hot filling evenly into the crust and top evenly with the meringue, making swirls on the surface with the back of a spoon. Return the pie to the oven and bake until the meringue is golden brown, about 15 minutes.

11 Let cool for 1 hour, then refrigerate for at least 3 hours or up to 24 hours, before cutting into wedges to serve.

12 Refrigerate leftovers, tightly wrapped, for up to 1 day.

In the fall, I enjoy picking apples—or, as Joe says, *overpicking* them, because I tend to go a little crazy—and every year I create new recipes—both sweet and savory—to use them. But no matter how far and wide I expand my repertoire, I always find myself coming back to this classic. On a cold November day, nothing is as warming as a bowl of this apple crisp. For the full experience, scoop the best-quality vanilla ice cream you can get your hands on over the top and watch it gently melt into the sticky toffee sauce before digging in.

To make ahead, assemble the crumble and refrigerate, tightly covered with plastic wrap, for up to eight hours. Let it stand at room temperature for thirty minutes before baking.

Toffee Apple Crumble

1 Preheat the oven to 400°F. Butter a 9-inch pie pan and put it on a rimmed baking sheet.

2 Make the filling: Put the sliced apples, lemon juice, and cinnamon in a bowl. Stir to coat the apples.

3 Put a large (approximately 10-inch) skillet with high sides over medium heat. Add the 4 tablespoons butter and the brown sugar and heat until melted and bubbly. Add the apples and any juices that have collected in the bowl.

4 Cook, stirring frequently, for 5 minutes. Sprinkle the flour evenly over the apples and cook, stirring, for 1 minute longer. Spread the apples evenly in the prepared pan.

5 Mix the topping: Stir together the oats, flour, vanilla sugar, and salt in a bowl. Add the butter and use a pastry cutter or a fork to break up and distribute the butter evenly. Sprinkle the topping evenly over the apples.

6 Bake the crisp until the apples are tender and the top is golden brown, 40 to 45 minutes. Let cool for at least 20 minutes before serving warm or at room temperature.

FILLING

4 tablespoons (½ stick) unsalted butter, plus more for the pan

5 Granny Smith apples, peeled and cut into ½-inch-thick slices

Juice of ½ lemon

¾ teaspoon ground cinnamon

⅔ cup (packed) light brown sugar

2 tablespoons all-purpose flour

TOPPING

¾ cup oats

½ cup all-purpose flour

¼ cup vanilla sugar, or ¼ cup sugar plus ½ teaspoon pure vanilla extract

¼ teaspoon salt

4 tablespoons (½ stick) cold unsalted butter, cut into ½-inch cubes

¼ teaspoon ground cinnamon

Drizzled with tart, saucy jam and slathered with velvety, orange-scented whipped cream, this tender, buttery cake is perfect with an afternoon cup of coffee and, most important, good company.

Yellow Cake with Raspberry Jam & Orange Whipped Cream

JAM

2 cups fresh raspberries

1½ tablespoons granulated sugar

1 tablespoon freshly squeezed orange juice

CAKE

Nonstick cooking spray

2¾ cups all-purpose flour

2½ teaspoons baking powder

½ teaspoon salt

16 tablespoons (2 sticks) unsalted butter, softened

¾ cup granulated sugar

4 large eggs

1 tablespoon vanilla bean paste, or seeds scraped from 2 vanilla beans

1 cup whole milk

1 Make the jam: Heat the berries, sugar, and orange juice in a small saucepan over medium heat until the berries release some of their juices but still retain their shape, 2 to 3 minutes. Use a wooden spoon to smash the berries against the side of the pan, breaking them up into small pieces but leaving some texture. Transfer the jam to a bowl, cover with plastic wrap, and refrigerate until completely cool, about 2 hours.

2 Make the cake: Preheat the oven to 350°F. Spray a 10-cup Bundt pan with nonstick cooking spray.

3 In a small bowl, whisk together the flour, baking powder, and salt.

4 In the bowl of a stand mixer fitted with the paddle attachment, beat the butter and sugar on medium speed until light and fluffy, about 2 minutes. Add the eggs and vanilla and mix 2 minutes longer. On low speed, add the flour mixture and mix until just combined. With the mixer running, add the milk in a slow stream. Mix just long enough to form a smooth batter and no longer.

5 Spread the batter evenly into the prepared pan, smoothing the top. Bake until a toothpick tests clean at the center and the cake springs back when gently pressed with a finger, 60 to 70 minutes. Let cool in the pan for 10 minutes, then invert the cake onto a wire rack to cool completely.

6 Make the whipped cream: Using a chilled bowl and beaters, whip the cream with the confectioners' sugar and orange zest until it forms semi-firm peaks.

7 Sift confectioner's sugar over the cake. Serve slices of cake topped with the raspberry jam, letting the juices soak into the cake, and a dollop of the whipped cream.

8 Store leftover cake in an airtight container at room temperature for up to 3 days. Refrigerate leftover jam in an airtight container for up to 1 week.

WHIPPED CREAM

1 cup heavy cream

2 tablespoons confectioners' sugar, plus more for finishing

½ teaspoon grated orange zest, or more to taste

Nothing caps off a Mexican fiesta quite like these cinnamon sugar–coated treats, hot from the fryer, dunked in rich, melted chocolate. Golden and crispy on the outside, incredibly light on the inside, they offer great texture as well as flavor. When I have churros on my mind, I can't concentrate on anything else.

Churros with Chocolate Dipping Sauce

CHURROS

1 tablespoon safflower oil, plus more for frying

½ cup plus 1 tablespoon sugar

1 tablespoon ground cinnamon

3 tablespoons unsalted butter

1 teaspoon pure vanilla extract

½ teaspoon salt

1 cup all-purpose flour

2 large eggs

SAUCE

1 cup semisweet chocolate chips

½ cup heavy cream

1 tablespoon light corn syrup

Pinch of salt

1 Make the churros: Put a Dutch oven over medium heat. Add enough oil to fill the pan halfway, and slowly heat it to 375°F. (Put the handle end of a wooden spoon into the oil; if the oil bubbles vigorously around the handle, it's ready.)

2 Meanwhile, in a shallow bowl, stir together ½ cup of the sugar and the cinnamon. Line a plate with paper towels. Put the cinnamon sugar and the plate near the stove.

3 In a 2-quart saucepan, stir together the butter, vanilla, salt, 1 tablespoon oil, the remaining 1 tablespoon of sugar, and 1 cup water. Bring to a boil, then reduce the heat to low, and add the flour, stirring constantly until the mixture forms a ball. Continue to cook and stir for 1 minute longer.

4 Transfer the dough to the bowl of stand mixer fitted with a paddle attachment and mix for 1 minute to slightly cool the mixture. Add the eggs, one at a time, mixing well after each addition.

5 Spoon the dough into a pastry bag fitted with a large star tip (Ateco #824).

6   Check that the oil is at temperature, then carefully pipe the dough into the hot oil, snipping it into 5-inch ropes with kitchen shears as you pipe. Working in batches to avoid crowding them, continue to form and fry the churros until they are deep golden brown all over, 4 to 5 minutes.

7   As they are ready, use a long-handled wire-mesh strainer (spider) to retrieve the churros, holding them over the pot for a moment to let most of the oil drain before transferring them to the paper towel–lined plate. After 2 minutes, roll the hot churros in the cinnamon sugar, then transfer them to a serving plate.

8   Make the chocolate sauce: Put the chocolate chips in a small bowl. Heat the cream to simmering in a small saucepan, then pour it over the chocolate. Let stand for a minute or two, then whisk until smooth and creamy. Whisk in the corn syrup and salt.

9   Serve the hot churros with the sauce for dipping.

My nonna always adds a shot of marsala or rum to her tiramisù. Taking a page from her book, I like to change up the liqueur, too, based on my mood. This version, inspired by flavored coffee, may just be my favorite. Sweet, boozy, and oh-so-nutty, it may be even better than the classic. Use a good-quality Italian mascarpone, such as Galbani or Cinque Stelle brand. For the *savoiardi,* my favorite brand is Bellino.

Hazelnut Tiramisù

4 large egg yolks

½ cup plus 2 tablespoons sugar

1 cup heavy cream

1 pound mascarpone cheese, softened

1 teaspoon pure vanilla extract

¾ cup Frangelico or other hazelnut-flavored liqueur

1¼ cups freshly brewed coffee

34 to 45 *savoiardi* cookies (ladyfingers)

Unsweetened cocoa powder

½ cup hazelnuts, toasted and coarsely chopped

1   In a bowl, using a stand mixer, beat the egg yolks with ¼ cup of the sugar until they are thick, pale, and about doubled in volume.

2   Using a chilled bowl and beaters, whip the cream until firm peaks form.

3   In a medium bowl, use a wooden spoon or spatula to mix the mascarpone cheese, ¼ cup of the sugar, and the vanilla. Add the egg yolk mixture and ¼ cup of the Frangelico until combined. Fold in the whipped cream.

4   In a shallow bowl, stir together the coffee, the remaining 2 tablespoons sugar, and the remaining ½ cup Frangelico.

5   To assemble the tiramisù, dunk the *savoiardi,* one at a time, into the coffee mixture on both sides, transferring them to an 8 × 12 × 3-inch baking pan as you go, until you have entirely covered the bottom of the pan in a single layer. Spread half of the cream mixture over the layer of *savoiardi* and sift cocoa powder generously over the top.

6   Make another layer in the same manner, with a single layer of coffee-dipped *savoiardi,* the remaining cream mixture, and cocoa. Scatter the chopped hazelnuts over the top.

7   Cover tightly with plastic wrap and refrigerate for at least 6 hours or overnight before scooping out servings.

Make this addictive tart for someone you really like, because chances are they will be coming around more often, unable to stop thinking about their next encounter with it. With a buttery crust, thick caramel, and glossy chocolate ganache, this tart is a decadent work of art—yet the crust is a couldn't-be-simpler press-in-the-pan one, and the caramel filling, store-bought dulce de leche.

Caramel & Chocolate Shortbread Tart

CRUST

8 tablespoons (1 stick) unsalted butter, softened

¼ cup confectioners' sugar

1 teaspoon pure vanilla extract

1½ cups all-purpose flour

¼ teaspoon salt

FILLING

1 (13.4 ounce) can dulce de leche, such as La Lechera

GANACHE

6 ounces semisweet chocolate chips

¼ cup heavy cream

1 tablespoon unsalted butter, softened

⅛ teaspoon salt

1 Make the crust: Preheat the oven to 350°F.

2 In the bowl of a stand mixer fitted with the paddle attachment, beat the butter with the confectioners' sugar and vanilla on medium speed for 1 minute. Add the flour and salt and mix to combine.

3 Press the crust into a 9-inch round tart pan with a removable bottom. Line the crust with foil, shiny side down, and fill with dried beans or rice to prevent the crust from puffing or shrinking. Put the pan on a baking sheet and bake for 15 minutes, then remove the foil and beans and return the crust to the oven until it is light golden, about 10 minutes longer. Set aside to cool.

4 Spread the dulce de leche evenly over the crust. Cover the tart with plastic wrap and refrigerate until cold, about 4 hours or up to 24 hours.

5 About an hour before serving, make the ganache: Put the chocolate chips in a bowl. Heat the cream to just below a boil in a small saucepan. Pour the cream over the chocolate and wait 1 minute to let the chocolate melt. Whisk until smooth and then whisk in the butter and salt.

6 Pour the ganache over the caramel and smooth the top with an offset spatula or the back of a spoon. Refrigerate the tart until the ganache is set, about 1 hour or up to 8 hours. If chilled for more than an hour, let it stand at room temperature for 30 minutes before serving.

7 To serve, cut the tart into wedges, wiping your knife clean with a damp kitchen towel between cuts for the neatest slices.

8 Refrigerate leftovers, tightly wrapped, for up to 3 days.

This delicious cheesecake is quite possibly the world's easiest version of what can often be a finicky dessert. I know it's my favorite, as there's no need to worry about water baths, cooking times, or the top cracking. Prepare a day ahead, as it needs a night in the fridge to set.

The cheesecake can be refrigerated, tightly wrapped in its springform pan (avoid letting the wrap touch the top of the cake), up to three days ahead.

No-Bake Nutella Cheesecake

1 Make the crust: Process the hazelnuts in a food processor until finely ground. Add the cracker crumbs, sugar, butter, and Nutella and process until well mixed and the mixture holds together when you pinch it between your fingers. Press into the bottom and 1 inch up the sides of a 9-inch round springform pan.

2 Prepare the filling: In the bowl of a stand mixer fitted with the paddle attachment, mix the cream cheese and Nutella on medium speed for 2 minutes. Add the sugar, cream, and vanilla and mix until completely smooth, about 3 minutes longer. Spread the filling evenly into the crust. Cover the pan with an inverted plate and refrigerate overnight.

3 About 1 hour before serving, make the ganache. Put the chocolate chips in a small bowl. Heat the cream to just below a boil in a small saucepan. Pour the cream over the chocolate, wait 1 minute, and then whisk until smooth. Whisk in the butter until completely incorporated.

4 Spread the warm ganache evenly over the filling with an offset spatula or the back of a spoon. Cover the pan again with the plate and refrigerate to set the ganache, at least 1 hour or overnight.

5 Remove the sides from the springform pan, leaving the cheesecake on the base. Top with the chopped hazelnuts and sift confectioners' sugar over all. Cut the cheesecake into wedges, wiping the knife clean with a kitchen towel between slices.

CRUST

¼ cup hazelnuts, coarsely chopped

1¼ cups graham cracker crumbs

¼ cup granulated sugar

6 tablespoons (¾ stick) unsalted butter, softened

2 tablespoons Nutella

FILLING

2 8-ounce packages cream cheese, softened

1½ cups Nutella

½ cup confectioners' sugar

¼ cup heavy cream

½ teaspoon pure vanilla extract

GANACHE

4 ounces semisweet chocolate chips

⅓ cup heavy cream

1 teaspoon unsalted butter, softened

⅓ cup coarsely chopped toasted hazelnuts

Confectioners' sugar

This is the most chocolaty chocolate cake you will ever taste. The frosting is like a melted candy bar and the interior has a moist, tender crumb. This cake is so good, it should be illegal, but the cake police haven't caught up with me yet! If you can resist devilishly devouring the entire cake immediately (alone or with help), this one stores well at room temperature, either covered with plastic wrap or in an airtight container.

Devilishly Good Devil's Food Cake

GANACHE

1 (15-ounce) bag semisweet chocolate chips

1⅓ cups heavy cream

CAKE

Nonstick cooking spray

⅓ cup whole milk

1 tablespoon instant coffee granules

2¼ cups all-purpose flour

¾ cup Dutch-process unsweetened cocoa powder

2 teaspoons baking soda

1 teaspoon baking powder

1 teaspoon salt

16 tablespoons (2 sticks) unsalted butter, softened

2 cups sugar

3 large eggs

1 teaspoon pure vanilla extract

1 Make the ganache: Put the chocolate chips in a small bowl. Heat the cream to just below a boil in a small saucepan. Pour the cream over the chocolate, wait for 1 minute, and then whisk until smooth. Set the ganache aside, covering it tightly with plastic wrap once it reaches room temperature to prevent a skin from forming.

2 Make the cake: Preheat the oven to 350°F. Spray two 9-inch round cake pans with nonstick cooking spray and line the bottoms with parchment paper rounds. Spray the paper.

3 In a small saucepan, stir together the milk, coffee granules, and 1 cup water. Bring to a simmer, then remove from the heat and let cool slightly.

4 In a bowl, whisk together the flour, cocoa, baking soda, baking powder, and salt.

5 In the bowl of a stand mixer fitted with the paddle attachment, beat the butter and sugar on medium speed until light and fluffy, about 2 minutes. Add the eggs and vanilla, mixing until well combined.

6 Add half of the flour mixture and half of the cooled coffee mixture. Mix on low until just combined. Add the remaining flour mixture and coffee mixture, mixing until just incorporated.

7   Divide the batter evenly between the prepared pans and smooth the tops. Tap the pans lightly on the counter to remove any air bubbles.

8   Bake until a toothpick tests clean at the center and the cake springs back when gently pressed with a finger, 30 to 35 minutes. Let cool in the pans for 10 minutes, then invert the cakes onto a wire rack to cool completely.

9   To assemble, line the edges of a cake stand with parchment paper, then put one layer of cake upside down on the stand. Spread one-quarter of the ganache evenly over the surface of the cake. Put the second layer on top of the first, top side up. Spread the remaining ganache all over the top and sides of the cake.

10 Cut the cake into wedges, and serve.

When I make egg yolk pasta from scratch, you can expect a pavlova for dessert because the idea of throwing away the whites makes me cringe. This showstopper of a dessert puts them to great use, with a crunchy-chewy meringue base supporting piles of cream and fruit. You can use any combination of fruit you like, but do make sure it has a good sweet-tart balance.

To make ahead, store the cooled meringue at room temperature, tightly wrapped in plastic wrap, for up to one day. Once filled with cream and fruit, the pavlova may be refrigerated, lightly covered with plastic wrap, for a few hours before serving.

Stunning Pavlova

1 Make the meringue: Preheat the oven to 300°F. Using a 9-inch pie plate as a guide, draw a circle with a pencil on a piece of parchment paper. Invert the parchment onto a baking sheet. (This avoids your pavlova touching the pencil markings.)

2 In the clean bowl of a stand mixer, using a clean whisk attachment, beat the egg whites until they are foamy. Add the cream of tartar and salt, then whip until the whites begin to form soft peaks. With the mixer running, gradually add in the sugar, 1 tablespoon at a time, pausing to incorporate each addition before adding the next. Continue to beat until the whites are thick and glossy and all of the sugar has dissolved. To test, rub a bit of meringue between your fingers. If it feels gritty, continue beating until it feels completely smooth.

3 Use a spatula to gently fold in the cornstarch, vinegar, and vanilla by hand, taking care not to deflate the whites.

4 Put a dab of meringue under each corner of the parchment paper to anchor the paper to the pan. Scrape the rest of the meringue onto the center of the circle, and use a spoon or an offset spatula to spread it into an even 9-inch circle, making a slight indentation in the center to hold the filling.

(recipe continues)

MERINGUE

5 large egg whites, at room temperature

½ teaspoon cream of tartar

¼ teaspoon salt

1 cup superfine sugar

2 teaspoons cornstarch

1 teaspoon white wine vinegar or balsamic vinegar

½ teaspoon pure vanilla extract

RASPBERRY SYRUP

½ cup seedless raspberry jam

1 tablespoon fresh orange juice

1 teaspoon orange zest

CREAM

1 cup heavy cream

2 tablespoons confectioners' sugar

4 cups mixed berries

5 Bake the meringue until the surface is dry to the touch, about 50 minutes. Leaving the pavlova inside, turn the oven off and leave the door ajar until the pavlova has cooled completely, about 3 hours. (Don't worry that the pavlova will look dry and cracked; the interior will have a lovely marshmallow texture.)

6 Prepare the syrup: Heat the jam, orange juice, and zest over medium heat until warm and runny, about 1 minute. Set aside to cool slightly.

7 Whip the cream: In a bowl, whip the heavy cream until it forms soft peaks. Add the sugar and continue whipping until firm peaks form.

8 Gently slide a spatula under the pavlova and transfer it to a serving platter. Spoon the cream into the center and spread it evenly. Scatter the berries over the top, then drizzle the syrup over all. Cut into wedges, and serve.

The first time I experienced a red velvet cupcake was at a child's birthday party. I wasn't sure what to expect of the little red cakes, and for the longest time, I couldn't describe them. What I did know was that I was hooked on those chocolate-kissed vanilla cakes. Paired with a rich cream cheese frosting, these babies are sure to be a hit at your table.

Red Velvet Cupcakes

1   Make the cupcakes: Preheat the oven to 350°F. Line a muffin pan with 12 cupcake liners.

2   In a small bowl, whisk together the flour, cocoa, baking powder, baking soda, and salt. In the bowl of a stand mixer fitted with the paddle attachment at medium speed, beat the butter and sugar until creamy and light. Mix in the egg and vanilla until well combined. With the mixer on low, mix in the buttermilk, vinegar, and food coloring. Add the flour mixture and mix until combined.

3   Use an ice cream scoop or ¼-cup measure to divide the batter evenly among the muffin cups. Bake until a toothpick tests clean in the center of a cupcake, 18 to 22 minutes. Let cool for 5 minutes in the pan before transferring the cupcakes in their liners directly to a wire rack to cool completely.

4   Mix the frosting: Put the cream cheese, butter, sugar, milk, and vanilla in a bowl and beat with a stand mixer until creamy.

5   Frost the cupcakes with a small offset spatula. Alternatively, transfer the frosting to a pastry bag fitted with a plain large tip and pipe onto the cupcakes.

6   Refrigerate the cupcakes for 10 to 15 minutes to set the frosting before serving. These cupcakes are best the day they are made, but leftovers will hold up reasonably well if refrigerated in an airtight container for up to 2 days.

CUPCAKES

1¼ cups all-purpose flour

2 tablespoons Dutch-process cocoa powder

½ teaspoon baking powder

½ teaspoon baking soda

¼ teaspoon salt

4 tablespoons (½ stick) unsalted butter, softened

¾ cup granulated sugar

1 large egg

1 teaspoon pure vanilla extract

¾ cup buttermilk

1 teaspoon distilled white vinegar

1 teaspoon red food coloring

FROSTING

8 tablespoons cream cheese, softened

2 tablespoons (¼ stick) unsalted butter, softened

2 cups confectioners' sugar

1 tablespoon milk

1 teaspoon pure vanilla extract

This *babà* holds a very special place in my heart because it was my maternal grandmother's favorite dessert. When my mother is feeling fancy, this is what she makes, serving it with thick whipped cream. It is the dessert she made for my husband, Joe, the very first time she met him. My only change from her formula is to reduce the rum to a more reasonable level. Choose a nice spicy dark rum here—the flavor needs to come through.

Mama's Babà al Rum

DOUGH

½ cup whole milk

1 tablespoon sugar

1 (¼-ounce) packet active dry yeast

3 large eggs

1¾ cups all-purpose flour

½ teaspoon salt

4 tablespoons (½ stick) unsalted butter, softened, plus more for the bowl and pan

RUM SYRUP

⅓ cup sugar

½ cup dark rum

Whipped cream

Maraschino cherries (optional)

1 Make the dough: Heat the milk in a small saucepan until it is warm (110°F to 115°F). Pour it into the bowl of a stand mixer, off the mixer, and whisk in the sugar and yeast. Let stand for 2 minutes. Add the eggs and whisk to combine.

2 Add the flour and salt, then put the bowl onto the mixer fitted with the paddle attachment and mix on low until the flour is moistened. Add the butter, 1 tablespoon at a time, letting each addition incorporate before adding the next.

3 Exchange the paddle attachment for the dough hook. Mix on medium speed to form a sticky dough, 4 to 5 minutes.

4 Butter a bowl and transfer the dough to the bowl. Cover with plastic wrap and let the dough rise until doubled in volume, about 1 hour.

5 Brush a babà pan (or a 5-cup tube pan) with melted butter. Gently run a spatula around the edge of the dough to deflate it a bit, then spread evenly in the pan. Cover with plastic wrap and let rise until the dough reaches the top of the pan, 30 to 45 minutes.

6 Preheat the oven to 350°F.

7 Gently slide the babà into the oven and bake until it is golden brown and a toothpick inserted into the center comes out clean, 35 to 40 minutes.

8 Meanwhile, make the rum syrup: In a small saucepan, stir the sugar with ½ cup water over medium heat until the sugar dissolves. Remove from the heat and stir in the rum. Let cool to room temperature.

9 Allow the babà to cool for 30 minutes, then invert it onto a platter that has a lip to catch the syrup. Slowly drizzle the syrup over the still-warm cake, allowing it to soak up the syrup.

10 Let the babà sit for at least 30 minutes before serving, or refrigerate, tightly wrapped, for up to 8 hours. (If the babà is not inclined to absorb it all, serve the remaining syrup in a pitcher on the side.) If refrigerated, let it stand for 30 minutes at room temperature before serving.

11 To serve, cut the babà into thick slices and spoon some of the syrup that has run off the babà onto the platter over the top. Garnish with a dollop of whipped cream, and a cherry, if you like!

12 Refrigerate leftover babà, tightly wrapped, for up to 3 days.

The unbeatable classic combination of sweet poached peaches filled with smooth, creamy ice cream is best enjoyed in midsummer, when peaches are the color of sunshine and raspberries are plump and juicy. Found on the juice aisle of most supermarkets, peach nectar enhances the peaches' sweet flavor.

To make ahead, refrigerate the poached peaches and raspberry sauce in separate airtight containers for up to two days.

Peach Melba

6 yellow peaches, ripe but still quite firm

⅓ cup granulated sugar

½ cup peach nectar

1 (3-inch) vanilla bean, split open

3 cups fresh raspberries

¼ cup confectioners' sugar

Juice of ½ lemon

1 pint vanilla ice cream

1   Cut each peach in half from stem-end to bottom, twisting to separate the halves and leaving the pit in one half of each peach.

2   To poach the peaches, put a 2-quart saucepan over medium heat. Add the sugar, peach nectar, vanilla bean, and 3 cups water. Bring the mixture to a boil, then simmer for 5 minutes. Put the peach halves into the poaching liquid, cut side down, and cook them for about 5 minutes, then turn and cook 3 minutes longer. Let the peaches cool in the poaching liquid to room temperature.

3   Meanwhile, process the raspberries, confectioners' sugar, and lemon juice in a blender or food processor until liquefied. Strain the mixture into a bowl through a fine-mesh strainer, pressing on the solids to extract all of the juices. (Discard any solids remaining in the strainer.)

4   To serve, remove the pits remaining in the peach halves. Use a paring knife to gently scrape away the skin; discard.

5   Put 2 peach halves, cut side up, in each of 6 serving bowls and top with a scoop of ice cream. Pour the raspberry sauce over the ice cream, and serve.

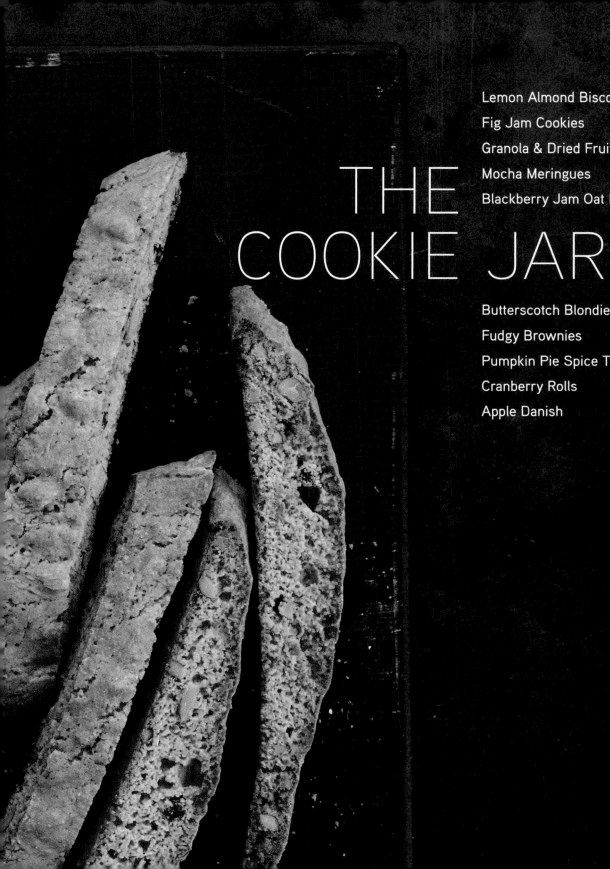

THE COOKIE JAR

Lemon Almond Biscotti

Fig Jam Cookies

Granola & Dried Fruit Bars

Mocha Meringues

Blackberry Jam Oat Bars

Butterscotch Blondies

Fudgy Brownies

Pumpkin Pie Spice Twists

Cranberry Rolls

Apple Danish

I grew up eating traditional anise *cantuccini* (the Italian term for this type of biscotti) and have been making variations of them forever. I love all things lemon, and this almond-studded version is one of my favorites. There is no better cookie for dunking into a cup of tea or espresso.

Lemon Almond Biscotti

1 cup raw almonds, coarsely chopped

3 cups all-purpose flour, plus more for shaping

1 teaspoon baking powder

½ teaspoon salt

8 tablespoons (1 stick) unsalted butter, softened

1½ cups sugar

4 large eggs

2 teaspoons pure vanilla extract

Finely grated zest of 2 lemons

1. Position oven racks in the lower and upper third of the oven and preheat the oven to 350°F. Line 2 rimmed baking sheets with parchment paper.

2. Toast the almonds on a separate rimmed baking sheet in a single layer until they are light golden, about 10 minutes. Transfer to a plate and let cool completely.

3. In a bowl, whisk together the flour, baking powder, and salt to combine.

4. In the bowl of a stand mixer fitted with the paddle attachment, beat the butter and sugar on medium speed until light and fluffy, about 2 minutes. Mix in the eggs, vanilla, and lemon zest until combined. Add the flour mixture at low speed, mixing until just incorporated. Fold in the toasted almonds by hand to evenly incorporate them.

5. Transfer the dough to a generously floured surface and divide into 3 equal pieces. Use your hands to shape each piece into a 10-inch log.

6. Arrange two of the logs on one of the prepared baking sheets and one on the other, leaving about 4 inches all around the sides of each to allow for spreading. Gently flatten the logs with your hands until they are 2 inches wide.

7   Bake until the logs are light golden all over and firm to the
    touch near the center, 30 to 35 minutes, rotating the sheets
    front to back and top to bottom halfway through baking. Keep
    the oven on.

8   Let the logs cool on the sheets until they can be easily handled,
    about 10 minutes. Transfer to a cutting board and use a serrated
    knife to cut them on an angle into about ¾-inch-thick slices.

9   Arrange the biscotti with a cut side up on the lined baking
    sheets and bake for 7 minutes. Flip the biscotti, rotate the
    baking sheets front to back and top to bottom, and bake until
    golden all over, about 7 minutes longer.

10 Let cool for about 5 minutes on the sheets before transferring
    the biscotti to a wire rack to cool completely. Store leftover
    cookies in an airtight container for up to 1 week.

Growing up in Italy, we ate figs often fresh or dried. After moving to the U.S., I discovered the delicious store-bought fig cookies most Americans know and love. After years of buying them (I occasionally still do), I wanted to try making them from scratch. The lightly spiced, pillowy soft dough I've created makes a perfect blanket for holding the fig preserves.

Fig Jam Cookies

1¾ cups all-purpose flour, plus more for rolling

¼ teaspoon salt

⅛ teaspoon ground cinnamon

8 tablespoons (1 stick) unsalted butter, softened

¼ cup vegetable shortening

¼ cup granulated sugar

¼ cup (packed) light brown sugar

1 large egg

1 teaspoon pure vanilla extract

Finely grated zest of ½ orange

1 (10-ounce) jar fig preserves

1   In a small bowl, whisk together the flour, salt, and cinnamon.

2   In the bowl of a stand mixer fitted with the paddle attachment on medium-low speed, mix the butter, shortening, and granulated and brown sugars until well combined, about 2 minutes. Mix in the egg, vanilla, and orange zest. Add the flour mixture and mix until the dough just comes together.

3   Gather the dough into a ball and flatten into a disk. Wrap in plastic wrap and refrigerate for at least 1 hour or up to 8 hours.

4   Position oven racks in the upper and lower thirds of the oven and preheat the oven to 350°F. Line two rimmed baking sheets with parchment paper.

5   Roll out the dough on a well-floured surface into a 12 × 16-inch rectangle. Neatly trim the dough all around, then cut into strips crosswise to make 4 (12 × 4-inch) strips.

6   Spoon the preserves lengthwise down the center of each strip. Wet your finger with water and run it along both long sides of each strip. Fold one long side of each strip over the filling, then the other side, slightly overlapping them. Press to seal. Cut each strip crosswise into 8 pieces and arrange them, seam side down, with about 1 inch all around, on the prepared baking sheets.

7   Bake until the bottoms are light golden, about 15 minutes. Allow the cookies to cool for about 5 minutes on the sheets before transferring them to a wire rack to cool completely.

There's something very gratifying about making homemade snacks. I do occasionally purchase store-bought treats, but I prefer to make them myself so I can play with flavor combinations. For these, I've added dried fruit, for granola bars that are sweet, nutty, and chewy. Use whatever combination of nuts and fruits you like.

Granola & Dried Fruit Bars

1 Preheat the oven to 350°F. Line a 9-inch square baking pan with parchment paper and spray with nonstick cooking spray.

2 In a bowl, whisk together the oats, flour, baking soda, cinnamon, and salt. Stir in the almonds, walnuts, apricots, blueberries, and cherries.

3 In a small saucepan over medium heat, melt the butter with the honey and brown sugar. Bring to a boil, then stir in the vanilla off the heat. Pour the butter mixture into the oat mixture and mix well.

4 Spread the mixture evenly into the prepared pan and bake until golden brown, 40 to 45 minutes.

5 The bars hold together best when cut just slightly warm. Let cool for about 1 hour, then cut into 4 equal strips in one direction and 6 in the other, to make 24 bars. Store leftover bars in an airtight container for up to 1 week.

Nonstick cooking spray

2 cups old-fashioned rolled oats

⅓ cup all-purpose flour

½ teaspoon baking soda

¼ teaspoon ground cinnamon

⅛ teaspoon salt

½ cup slivered almonds

½ cup coarsely chopped walnuts

½ cup dried apricots, coarsely chopped

¼ cup dried blueberries

¼ cup dried cherries

8 tablespoons (1 stick) unsalted butter

⅔ cup honey

⅓ cup (packed) light brown sugar

½ teaspoon pure vanilla extract

I am a big coffee drinker (I'm Italian!) and I adore chocolate, so it's no surprise that I drool at anything mocha. These babies are not too sweet, so the chocolate and coffee flavors really come through.

Mocha Meringues

3 large egg whites, at room temperature

½ teaspoon cream of tartar

¼ teaspoon salt

⅔ cup superfine sugar

2 tablespoons Dutch-process cocoa powder

1 teaspoon instant coffee granules

2 tablespoons grated semisweet chocolate

1   Position oven racks in the upper and lower thirds of the oven and preheat the oven to 250°F. Line two rimmed baking sheets with parchment paper.

2   In a clean bowl, using a stand mixer with clean beaters on medium-high speed, beat the egg whites until they are frothy. Add the cream of tartar and salt, mixing until combined.

3   Add the sugar, a little bit at a time, mixing until the egg whites are thick and glossy and the sugar is fully dissolved. If you rub a bit of the mixture between your fingers, you should feel no graininess from the sugar; if you do, keep mixing.

4   Sift the cocoa and coffee over the whites. Add the chocolate and fold everything in.

5   Form 36 meringues, using two small spoons and about 1 tablespoon of the mixture for each, spacing them on the prepared sheets with 1 inch all around them. Or fill a pastry bag fitted with a large round tip and pipe out 2-inch meringues.

6   Bake for 1 hour 35 minutes, rotating the sheets front to back and top to bottom, halfway through baking. Turn the oven off with the door closed and the meringues inside and leave to cool and dry for 3 hours.

7   Store leftover meringues in an airtight container at room temperature for up to 2 weeks.

I have a soft spot for blackberry jam, which reminds me of my days as a child in Bacoli (Naples), where I would pick blackberries with my nonna. We would return to her kitchen with juice-stained hands to make the berries into jam, which I enjoyed on everything and anything, all year long. These buttery, crumbly bars are one of my favorite uses for any kind of jam, especially blackberry.

Blackberry Jam Oat Bars

1   Preheat the oven to 350°F. Spray a 9-inch square baking pan with nonstick cooking spray. Line the pan with two strips of parchment paper, arranging one lengthwise and the other crosswise so that flaps extend on all four sides.

2   In a small bowl, stir together the flour, oats, and salt.

3   In the bowl of a stand mixer fitted with the paddle attachment, mix the butter, cream cheese, and brown sugar on medium speed until light and fluffy, 2 minutes. Add the zest and vanilla. Add the flour mixture and mix on low until just combined.

4   Set aside ½ cup of the dough, and with lightly floured hands, press the rest evenly into the bottom of the prepared pan. Bake until light golden, about 15 minutes.

5   Meanwhile, in a small bowl, stir together the jam and orange juice.

6   Spread the jam mixture evenly over the baked oat base. Use 2 small spoons to drop bits of the reserved dough evenly over the top. Bake until the top is golden, about 25 minutes longer.

7   Let cool completely, about 3 hours, before cutting into 4 equal strips in one direction and 4 in the other, to make 16 bars. Store leftover bars in an airtight container for up to 2 days.

Nonstick cooking spray

1¼ cups all-purpose flour, plus more for shaping

1 cup quick-cooking rolled oats

¼ teaspoon salt

12 tablespoons (1½ sticks) unsalted butter, softened

4 tablespoons cream cheese, softened

½ cup (packed) light brown sugar

Finely grated zest of ½ orange or 1 clementine

1 teaspoon pure vanilla extract

¾ cup seedless blackberry jam

Juice of ½ orange

For the longest time, I used butterscotch chips only around the holidays. One day, while making a batch of my white chocolate chip blondies, I noticed an open bag of butterscotch chips left over from a holiday baking project and—never one to waste—thought I'd use them in my batter. The combination of the fluffy, slightly dense blondie and caramel-butterscotch flavor created magic. No more waiting for the holidays to enjoy this treat!

Butterscotch Blondies

1¼ cups all-purpose flour

1 teaspoon baking powder

¼ teaspoon salt

8 tablespoons (1 stick) unsalted butter, softened, plus more for the pan

¼ cup granulated sugar

⅓ cup (packed) light brown sugar

2 large eggs

1 teaspoon vanilla bean paste or pure vanilla extract

1 cup butterscotch chips

1　Preheat the oven to 350°F. Butter a 9-inch square baking pan and line the bottom with parchment paper.

2　In a bowl, whisk together the flour, baking powder, and salt.

3　In the bowl of a stand mixer fitted with the paddle attachment, beat together the butter, granulated sugar, and brown sugar on medium speed until light and creamy, about 2 minutes. Add the eggs and vanilla, and mix until smooth. Add the flour mixture and mix until just combined, then fold in the butterscotch chips.

4　Spread the batter evenly in the prepared pan and bake until a toothpick tests clean near the center, 25 to 30 minutes. Let cool in the pan for 15 minutes, then invert the blondie onto a wire rack and let cool completely, about 3 hours.

5　Cut into 4 equal strips in one direction and 4 in the other, to make 16 blondies. Store leftover blondies in an airtight container, with wax paper between the layers, for up to 3 days.

I'm kind of known for my fudgy brownies. If you prefer a cakey brownie, move along. These are deeply chocolate and fudgy all the way through, not a dry crumb in sight. The espresso powder intensifies the chocolate flavor without dominating it, but it's not essential; if coffee isn't your thing, leave it out. The real key to my brownies' sticky, yummy goodness: Don't overbake them. The brownies are ready when a few moist crumbs stick to the toothpick when you test them near the center.

Fudgy Brownies

1 Preheat the oven to 350°F. Butter an 8-inch square baking pan. Line the pan with two strips of parchment paper, arranging one lengthwise and the other crosswise so that flaps extend on all four sides.

2 In a bowl, whisk together the flour, cocoa, and salt.

3 In a large bowl, using a spatula or wooden spoon, beat together the butter and sugar until light and creamy. Add the eggs and vanilla and mix until everything is incorporated. Fold in the flour mixture until just combined, then fold in the espresso powder and chocolate.

4 Spread the batter evenly into the prepared pan and bake until a toothpick has just a few moist crumbs clinging to it when you test near the center, about 40 minutes. Let cool in the pan for 15 minutes, then use the parchment strips to lift the brownie onto a wire rack and let it cool completely, about 3 hours.

5 Cut into 4 equal strips in one direction and 4 in the other, to make 16 brownies. Store leftover brownies in an airtight container, with wax paper between the layers, for up to 3 days.

⅔ cup all-purpose flour

1 tablespoon Dutch-process cocoa powder

¼ teaspoon salt

8 tablespoons (1 stick) unsalted butter, softened, plus more for the pan

1 cup sugar

2 large eggs

2 teaspoons pure vanilla extract

1 teaspoon instant espresso powder

1 cup bittersweet chocolate chips, melted

I can't imagine life without puff pastry—I use it for breakfast pockets, to top chicken potpies, and here, where a sprinkling of spiced sugar turns it into a quick sweet treat. The mixture of pumpkin pie spices and orange zest will fill your house with the scent of a fancy bakery. Nobody needs to know just how easily these are made.

Pumpkin Pie Spice Twists

2 tablespoons sugar

¾ teaspoon pumpkin pie spice

½ teaspoon finely grated
orange zest

⅛ teaspoon salt

1 sheet puff pastry (about
10 × 15 inches), thawed

1 large egg, whisked with
1 tablespoon milk or water

1 Line a baking sheet with parchment paper.

2 In a small bowl, mix together the sugar, pumpkin pie spice, orange zest, and salt.

3 Carefully unfold the puff pastry sheet onto a lightly floured surface and use a floured rolling pin to roll it into an 11 × 15-inch rectangle.

4 Brush the surface of the puff pastry evenly with the egg wash, leaving about one-third of the wash for a final brushing. Sprinkle all of the spiced sugar evenly over the surface.

5 Using a sharp knife or a pizza cutter and a straightedge, cut the pastry crosswise into 1-inch strips, making 15 strips. Pick up one strip and twist one end clockwise a few turns while holding the other end still, allowing the pastry to loosely twist around itself like a corkscrew. Transfer to the baking sheet, leaving about 1 inch between the twists. Continue with the remaining strips, arranging them on the baking sheet as you finish them.

6 Brush the twists gently with more egg wash. Pop the baking sheet into the freezer for 15 minutes.

7 Meanwhile, preheat the oven to 400°F.

8 Bake the twists until light golden brown all over, about 20 minutes. Let cool on the sheet for at least 10 minutes before serving warm or at room temperature.

These are easy to make, yet impressive and oh-so-delicious dunked into a cup of hot coffee or tea. The sweet dough is studded with bits of tart cranberry, making for a nice contrast in flavor and texture. These rolls are perfect for the holiday season, when cranberries seem to take over an entire section of the grocery store. If you have leftover cranberry sauce in the fridge, you could use that as the filling.

Cranberry Rolls

1   Mix the dough: In a small saucepan or in the microwave, warm the milk to 110°F to 115°F. Stir in about 1 teaspoon of the sugar and all of the yeast. Set aside for a few minutes, until foamy.

2   In the bowl of a stand mixer, whisk together the egg, butter, vanilla, and the yeast mixture until just combined. Add the flour, salt, and the remaining sugar.

3   Fit the mixer with the dough hook and mix on medium speed to make a smooth dough, 3 to 4 minutes. The dough will be very sticky at this point, but refrain from adding additional flour, which will result in a dense, heavy roll.

4   Put the dough in a lightly buttered bowl, turn to coat, cover with plastic wrap, and let rise in a warm place until doubled, about 2 hours.

5   Meanwhile, make the filling: In a small saucepan, stir together the cranberries, sugar, orange zest, and orange juice. Cook over medium-low heat, partially covered, until the cranberries pop, 7 to 8 minutes. Transfer the filling to a bowl, cover, and refrigerate until completely cool.

6   Turn the dough out onto a well-floured surface and press down gently. Knead for a minute, then roll it out into a 10 × 16-inch rectangle. Spread the cranberry filling evenly over the surface of the dough.

(recipe continues)

DOUGH

½ cup whole milk

¼ cup sugar

1¼ teaspoons active dry yeast

1 large egg

2 tablespoons (¼ stick) unsalted butter, melted, plus more for the bowl and pan

½ teaspoon pure vanilla extract

2¼ cups all-purpose flour, plus more for rolling

½ teaspoon salt

FILLING

1 cup fresh cranberries

½ cup sugar

Finely grated zest and juice of 1 orange

2 tablespoons (¼ stick) unsalted butter, melted

2 tablespoons turbinado or raw sugar

7   Butter a 10-inch round metal pan. Cut the dough crosswise into 8 strips that are 2 inches wide.

8   Pick up a strip and wrap it around your two fingers, twisting as you go to make a knot. Slip the dough off your fingers and tuck the tail into the space left in the center from your fingers. Put the roll into the prepared pan. Form the remaining rolls in the same manner, arranging them evenly in the pan. (Forming the rolls will get messy, but don't worry—it will be worth it in the end!)

9   Brush the tops of the rolls with the melted butter and sprinkle the turbinado sugar over the tops. Cover the rolls with plastic wrap and let rise in a warm spot until doubled in volume, 20 to 30 minutes.

10 Meanwhile, preheat the oven to 350°F.

11 Bake the rolls until they are golden brown, about 25 minutes. Let cool about 20 minutes before serving warm. Store leftover rolls in an airtight container for up to 4 days. To serve, pop one in the microwave for about 30 seconds to slightly soften and warm it.

This is my quick and easy version of Danish pastry, using store-bought puff pastry in place of the traditional, more labor-intensive yeasted dough. I have made endless varieties of Danish this way. This cream-cheese-and-apple-filled version is my husband's favorite.

Apple Danish

1 Make the apple filling: In a small saucepan, cook the apples, granulated sugar, and brown sugar over medium heat until the apples soften, 6 to 8 minutes. Off the heat, stir in the cinnamon. Let cool completely.

2 Mix the cream cheese filling: In a small bowl, stir together the cream cheese, sugar, egg yolk, vanilla, and lemon zest.

3 Unfold one sheet of the puff pastry onto a floured surface and trim to make a 10-inch square. Cut the square in half in both directions to make 4 smaller squares. Repeat with the second sheet.

4 Dollop a rounded tablespoon of the cream cheese mixture in the center of each square. Use a slotted spoon to top each with apple mixture. Brush the edges of each pastry with egg wash. Pinch together 2 opposite corners of each pastry, then the other 2 opposite corners, leaving the sides open to allow steam to escape as it bakes. Put the pastries on a parchment-lined baking sheet. Refrigerate for 20 minutes.

5 Preheat the oven to 400°F.

6 Brush the tops of the pastries with egg wash. Bake the pastries until they are golden brown, 25 to 30 minutes. Let cool for at least a few minutes before serving.

APPLE FILLING

2 Granny Smith apples, peeled and cut into ¼-inch dice

2 tablespoons granulated sugar

2 tablespoons (packed) light brown sugar

½ teaspoon ground cinnamon

CREAM CHEESE FILLING

8 tablespoons cream cheese, softened

¼ cup granulated sugar

1 large egg yolk

1 teaspoon pure vanilla extract

1 teaspoon finely grated lemon zest

2 (10 × 15-inch) sheets frozen puff pastry, thawed

All-purpose flour

1 large egg, whisked with 1 tablespoon milk or water

Orange-Scented Fruit Salad with Honey Yogurt

Maple Nutty Granola

Baked Eggs

Blini with Smoked Salmon & Scrambled Eggs

One-Pan Eggy Breakfast

Breakfast Bruschetta

Italian Eggs Benedict

Breakfast Quesadillas

Potato & Pepper Hash

Pancetta & Fontina Quiche

EASY BREAKFASTS & BRUNCHES

Frisée Salad with Poached Eggs & Bacon Dressing

Savory Bread Pudding

Cheddar-Bacon Waffles

Banana-Walnut Muffins

Cinnamon Rolls

Homemade Italian Doughnuts

Dutch Baby with Lemon Mascarpone & Berries

Fluffy Chocolate Chip Pancakes

Meyer Lemon–Blueberry Scones

On a hot summer day, when fresh, colorful fruit is abundant, not much can beat a cooling fruit salad. My choice for summer is a combination of blueberries, blackberries, and peaches. In spring, I turn to pineapple, strawberries, and mango. I serve the salad over slightly sweetened, orange-scented yogurt, either as a side dish for a breakfast feast, or as breakfast all in itself. Use a honey whose flavor you really like—the taste will shine through.

Orange-Scented Fruit Salad with Honey Yogurt

1   Put the orange zest in a small bowl, cover, and set aside.

2   Put the fruit in a bowl and mix in the orange juice and vanilla sugar. Cover and refrigerate for at least 1 hour or up to 8 hours.

3   At serving time, stir together the yogurt, honey, and reserved zest in a bowl.

4   To serve, spoon the fruit salad into four bowls and divide the honey yogurt over each serving. Sprinkle the mint leaves over the top, and serve.

5   Refrigerate leftover fruit and yogurt in separate airtight containers for up to 2 days.

Finely grated zest and juice of 1 orange

4 cups cubed assorted fresh fruit

3 tablespoons vanilla sugar, or 3 tablespoons sugar plus ¼ teaspoon pure vanilla extract

1¼ cups unsweetened whole-milk Greek yogurt

3 tablespoons orange blossom or clover honey, or to taste

4 to 6 fresh mint leaves, torn into pieces

I adore spending my weekends cooking and baking foods we can enjoy all through the week. Granola is one of my favorite weekend projects because it allows me to use up bits and pieces from my pantry, making it a little different each time. During the week, it's great to have the granola on hand, not only to start the morning in a bowl with milk, but also to scoop up while running out the door, or to curb my mid-afternoon sweet tooth. It's like snacking on crunchy cookie bites, only healthy! The combination I'm sharing here is my favorite, sweetened with maple syrup, spiced with cinnamon and vanilla, and speckled with an assortment of nuts and dried fruits for a little something different in every bite.

Maple Nutty Granola

½ cup safflower oil

½ cup maple syrup

1 teaspoon pure vanilla extract

¾ teaspoon ground cinnamon

¼ teaspoon salt

4 cups old-fashioned rolled oats

1½ cups sliced almonds

1 cup coarsely chopped walnuts

¼ cup (packed) light brown sugar

1 cup dried cranberries

½ cup dark raisins

½ cup golden raisins

1 Preheat the oven to 300°F.

2 In a medium bowl, whisk together the oil, maple syrup, vanilla, cinnamon, and salt. Add the oats, almonds, walnuts, and brown sugar and mix everything together well.

3 Spread out the mixture in a single layer on a rimmed baking sheet. Bake until deeply toasted and crispy, 45 to 50 minutes, stirring with a spatula every 10 minutes to brown everything evenly.

4 Remove the pan from the oven and stir in the cranberries and dark and golden raisins. Let cool completely. Store in an airtight container at room temperature for up to 1 week.

These eggs couldn't get any easier, but cooking them in individual ramekins makes them brunch worthy. (Ovenproof teacups make a pretty presentation in place of the ramekins, if you're feeling fancy.) Easily varied by adding small bits of ham, vegetables, or other cheeses to the ramekins before the eggs, these are so satisfying that I often make them for dinner for Joe and me, serving two eggs per person.

Baked Eggs

Unsalted butter

2 tablespoons heavy cream

4 large eggs

Salt and freshly ground black pepper

4 teaspoons freshly grated Parmigiano-Reggiano

¾ teaspoon Italian seasoning, homemade (page 14) or store-bought

1   Preheat the oven to 350°F. Butter 4 (6-ounce) ramekins and arrange them in a 9-inch square baking pan.

2   Divide the cream evenly among the ramekins. Crack an egg into each ramekin. Lightly season the eggs with salt and pepper. Sprinkle 1 teaspoon of parmigiano over each, and top with a pinch of the Italian seasoning.

3   Fill a kettle with hot water and pour water into the pan until it reaches halfway up the sides of the ramekins. Carefully transfer the pan to the oven and bake until the egg whites are set and the yolks are still runny, 15 to 18 minutes.

4   Carefully transfer each ramekin to a plate, and serve.

I like to make these for special occasions because they are such a showstopper, and a real treat. Buckwheat flour gives the blini a nutty flavor that goes so well with the delicate eggs and smoked salmon. My husband now expects these on special occasions, like Valentine's Day, or any morning when he feels the need for a special breakfast. That man is way too spoiled!

Blini with Smoked Salmon & Scrambled Eggs

BLINI

⅔ cup buckwheat flour

½ cup all-purpose flour

½ teaspoon dry mustard

½ teaspoon salt

1 cup warm whole milk
(110°F to 115°F)

2 teaspoons sugar

1 teaspoon rapid-rise yeast

2 large egg whites

2 large egg yolks

2 tablespoons (¼ stick)
unsalted butter, melted

3 to 4 tablespoons unsalted
butter, or more as needed

4 large eggs

¼ cup whole milk

Salt and freshly ground black
pepper

4 ounces smoked salmon

Chopped fresh chives

1 Make the blini: Sift the buckwheat and all-purpose flour with the mustard and salt into a bowl.

2 Stir the warm milk and sugar together in a small bowl. Sprinkle the yeast over the top, and let stand for about 2 minutes.

3 Meanwhile, use a standing mixer to whip the egg whites until they hold semi-firm peaks, taking care not to overbeat them.

4 Whisk the yeast mixture, egg yolks, and melted butter into the flour mixture just long enough to evenly combine the ingredients. Gently fold in the egg whites. Cover the bowl with a kitchen towel and leave in a warm place until doubled in volume, about 30 minutes.

5 To cook the blini, melt 1 tablespoon of the butter on a griddle or skillet over medium heat. Spoon ⅓ cup of the batter onto the hot griddle for each blini and cook until golden on both sides, about 2½ minutes on the first side and 1½ to 2 minutes on the second. Continue to make the blini, adding butter as needed to prevent sticking, and transferring the blini to a plate as you finish them. You should have 8 to 10 total. Cover the blini with aluminum foil to keep them warm while you prepare the eggs.

6   To cook the eggs, melt 2 tablespoons of the butter in a large
    skillet over medium-low heat.

7   In a bowl, whisk together the eggs, milk, and a pinch each of
    salt and pepper.

8   Pour the eggs into the pan and use a wooden spoon to
    constantly move them around in the pan as they gently cook.
    The eggs will cook quickly, so stay right by them, stirring, until
    they are firming up but are still luxuriously soft, or are done to
    your liking.

9   Serve 1 or 2 blini per plate, dividing the eggs and smoked
    salmon among them. Sprinkle the tops with chives, and serve.

Just about everyone loves bacon and eggs for breakfast, but this recipe elevates those staples. Cooking them together in one pan makes prep and cleanup extra easy on the cook, and I like to bring this to the table and serve it family style. Substitute breakfast sausage or pancetta for the bacon, if you like. Either way, this is bound to be a crowd-pleaser.

One-Pan Eggy Breakfast

4 slices bacon

1 tablespoon olive oil

4 ounces cremini mushrooms, halved

1 cup grape or cherry tomatoes, halved

5 ounces baby spinach

Salt and freshly ground black pepper

4 large eggs

2 scallions, white and light green parts only, sliced thin

4 slices sourdough toast

1 Put a 12-inch skillet over medium heat. Cook the bacon until crispy, about 3 minutes on each side. Transfer to a paper towel–lined plate to drain. Discard any bacon fat left behind in the skillet.

2 Raise the heat to medium-high, add the oil, wait 1 minute, then add the mushrooms and tomatoes. Cook, stirring frequently, until the mushrooms develop some color, about 3 minutes. Add the spinach and season with a pinch of salt and a few grinds of pepper. Cook, stirring frequently, until the spinach wilts, about 1 minute. Reduce the heat to medium-low.

3 Push the vegetables to the side and add the eggs to the cleared area in the pan. Cook until the whites are set and the yolks are still runny, about 3 minutes, or to your desired doneness.

4 Sprinkle salt and pepper lightly over the eggs. Arrange the bacon slices around the pan, and sprinkle the chopped scallions over everything. Serve family style, with the toast.

Put just about anything on toasted bread and it'll make me happy! This combination is so simple, it's hard to believe it's this good. The toasty bread, creamy avocado, smoky bacon, and oozy eggs are a match made in food heaven.

Breakfast Bruschetta

1   In a small bowl, mash the avocado with the lemon juice and parsley. Add salt and pepper to taste.

2   Heat a small skillet over medium-high heat. Add the bacon and cook until crisp, 2 to 3 minutes on each side. Transfer the bacon to a paper towel–lined plate to drain.

3   To poach the eggs, put a 1½-quart saucepan over medium heat and add water to reach about halfway up the sides. Bring to a simmer and stir in the vinegar.

4   One at a time, break the eggs into a small bowl and carefully tip them into the gently simmering water. When all four eggs are in, turn off the heat, cover the pan, and set a timer for 3½ minutes for runny yolks, 5 minutes for firmer ones.

5   Meanwhile, toast the bread and divide among 4 plates. Spread the mashed avocado over the toast slices. Crumble the bacon and sprinkle it over the avocado.

6   When the eggs are ready, remove them, one at a time, with a slotted spoon, gently dabbing them with a kitchen towel to soak up excess water, and put one on top of each prepared toast.

7   Sprinkle the tops with a little salt and pepper, and dig in.

1 ripe avocado

½ teaspoon fresh lemon juice

1 tablespoon finely chopped flat-leaf parsley

Salt and freshly ground black pepper

4 slices turkey bacon

1½ tablespoons distilled white vinegar

4 large eggs

4 slices sourdough bread

Eggs Benedict are a classic for good reason, but I love them even more with an Italian accent. So I've substituted buttered and toasted airy ciabatta for the English muffin, salty prosciutto for the ham, and tucked in some arugula for spicy flavor and vibrant color. The sauce? I wouldn't even contemplate trying to improve on a classic hollandaise!

Italian Eggs Benedict

HOLLANDAISE

2 large egg yolks

2 teaspoons fresh lemon juice

5 tablespoons unsalted butter, melted

Salt and cayenne pepper

1½ tablespoons distilled white vinegar

4 large eggs

4 slices ciabatta, sourdough, or other crusty bread

Unsalted butter

4 slices prosciutto

Handful of baby arugula

1 Make the hollandaise: Bring 1 inch of water to a gentle simmer in a 2-quart saucepan; keep warm over low heat.

2 Choose a nonreactive metal bowl that fits snugly when nested over the saucepan. Whisk the egg yolks and lemon juice vigorously in the bowl (not over the saucepan) until pale in color and about double in volume; about 3 minutes.

3 Nest the bowl over the saucepan of simmering water and continue to whisk constantly as you drizzle in the melted butter in a slow stream. Whisk until the sauce thickens enough to coat the back of a spoon, about 3 minutes. When you spoon some up and drop it back into the sauce, it should fall back on itself in a ribbon before disappearing into the sauce.

4 Remove the sauce from the heat and stir in a pinch each of salt and cayenne. Set the bowl aside off the heat, reserving the hot water in the saucepan for thinning the sauce before serving.

5 To poach the eggs, put a 1½-quart saucepan over medium heat and add water to reach about halfway up the sides. Bring to a simmer and stir in the vinegar.

6 One at a time, break the eggs into a small bowl and carefully tip them into the gently simmering water. When all 4 eggs are in, turn off the heat, cover the pan, and set a timer for 3½ minutes for runny yolks, 5 minutes for firmer ones.

7   While the eggs poach, spread a little butter on both sides of each bread slice. Toast the bread on both sides on a hot griddle or grill pan. Transfer each toast slice to a plate.

8   Warm the prosciutto on the griddle, about 1 minute per side. Lay 1 piece of prosciutto over each toast slice, and top each with a few arugula leaves.

9   When the eggs are ready, remove them, one at a time, with a slotted spoon, gently dabbing them with a kitchen towel to soak up excess water. Put 1 egg on top of each prepared toast.

10 To finish, check the hollandaise sauce. If it is too thick to run off the spoon when held over the bowl, whisk in the reserved hot water, a teaspoon at time, until it has a pourable consistency. Spoon hollandaise over each egg, and serve.

I can vividly remember the morning I made these for the first time. I had cooked up a Mexican-style fiesta the night before and had some spicy black beans left over, along with a little salsa. Being the self-proclaimed queen of leftovers, I decided on quesadillas filled with gooey cheese. Eggs helped to stretch everything out, and a star was born. Now, when I cook black beans, I purposely make extra just to make this the following day.

Breakfast Quesadillas

2 tablespoons safflower oil, plus more for brushing the tortillas

5 scallions, white and light green parts only, sliced thin

½ red bell pepper, cut into ¼-inch dice

½ jalapeño pepper, seeded and minced

¾ cup canned black beans, rinsed and drained

½ teaspoon ground cumin

4 (8-inch) flour tortillas

½ cup shredded Monterey Jack, pepper Jack, or sharp Cheddar cheese

6 large eggs

Salt and freshly ground black pepper

¼ cup coarsely chopped fresh cilantro

1   Put a large (approximately 10-inch) nonstick skillet over medium heat. Add the oil and let it get hot. Add the scallions, bell and jalapeño peppers, and beans, along with a small pinch of salt. Cook until the vegetables soften, about 5 minutes. Add the cumin and cook for a few seconds longer.

2   While the vegetables cook, lay the tortillas flat on a work surface and brush the tops lightly with oil. Flip them, oiled-side down, and sprinkle about 1 tablespoon of cheese over half of each tortilla.

3   Whisk the eggs in a small bowl with a pinch each of salt and pepper. Add the eggs to the skillet with the vegetables and cook, stirring constantly, until softy scrambled. Remove from the heat and stir in the cilantro.

4   Divide the egg mixture on top of the cheese. Sprinkle the remaining cheese over the eggs. Fold the empty halves of the tortillas over the filling.

5   Wipe the skillet out with a paper towel and put two quesadillas in the skillet. Cook over medium heat until the cheese melts and the tortillas are golden brown on both sides, about 3 minutes per side, flipping them halfway. Cook the remaining quesadillas in the same fashion, and serve.

A good recipe for hash browns is indispensable for turning eggs into something special when the weekend rolls around. With potatoes that are crispy on the outside and tender within, and with color and flavor from bell pepper and onion, this hash is ready to transform eggs into a hearty meal at any time of day.

Potato & Pepper Hash

1 Put a large (approximately 12-inch) nonstick skillet over medium heat. Add the oil and butter and let the pan get hot. Add the potatoes, tossing to coat them in the fat. Cover and cook for 10 minutes.

2 Remove the cover and increase the heat to medium-high. Add the onion and bell pepper, pressing them into a single layer, as much as possible, to encourage browning. Let the vegetables cook, turning them occasionally, until they are golden brown all over, about 15 minutes.

3 Reduce the heat to medium-low, add the garlic and parsley, season to taste with salt and pepper, and cook for 3 minutes longer. Serve immediately.

3 tablespoons olive oil

1 tablespoon unsalted butter

4 large or 6 medium russet potatoes (about 1½ pounds), peeled and cut into ½-inch cubes

1 large onion, cut into ½-inch dice

1 red bell pepper, cut into ½-inch dice

3 garlic cloves, minced

2 teaspoons coarsely chopped flat-leaf parsley

Salt and freshly ground black pepper

Pancetta lends a mouthwatering saltiness to this quiche. But because it's not smoked, it doesn't overpower the delicate nutty flavor of the fontina. Together, the two give this classic French dish an Italian spin. My secret for the flakiest crust ever: Freeze the flour for half an hour to get it super-chilled before mixing the dough.

Pancetta & Fontina Quiche

CRUST

1½ cups all-purpose flour, frozen for 30 minutes

½ teaspoon salt

5 tablespoons cold unsalted butter, cut into cubes

¼ cup cold vegetable shortening, cut into cubes

3 to 5 tablespoons ice water

Nonstick cooking spray

FILLING

6 ounces pancetta, cut into ½-inch pieces

2 scallions, white and light green parts only, coarsely chopped

5 large eggs

⅓ cup heavy cream

1 teaspoon granulated garlic

Salt and freshly ground black pepper

½ cup shredded fontina cheese

1 Make the crust: Briefly pulse the flour and salt in a food processor. Add the butter and shortening and pulse until they are the size of peas. Drizzle the ice water evenly over the mixture, starting with 3 tablespoons and adding more if needed, and pulse until the dough holds together when you pinch it between your fingers. (The crust can also be prepared in a standing mixer fitted with the paddle attachment.)

2 Turn the dough out onto a lightly floured work surface and, without handling it more than necessary, press it into a flat disk. Wrap the dough in plastic wrap and refrigerate for at least 30 minutes or overnight.

3 Preheat the oven to 400°F. Spray a 9-inch tart pan with nonstick cooking spray and put it on a baking sheet.

4 Roll out the crust on a floured surface into a 12-inch round. Transfer the crust to the prepared pan and settle it into the bottom and sides of the pan. Trim away any overhang from the edges. Line the crust with foil, shiny side down, and fill with dried beans or rice to prevent the crust from puffing or shrinking. Bake for 15 minutes, then remove the foil and beans and return the crust to the oven until it is light golden, about 10 minutes longer. Set the crust aside. Leave the oven on.

5 Prepare the filling: Put a large (approximately 10-inch) skillet over medium heat. Add the pancetta and cook until it begins to crisp, about 3 minutes. Add the scallions and cook 2 minutes longer. Transfer to a paper towel–lined plate with a slotted spoon.

6 In a large bowl, whisk together the eggs, cream, garlic, a good
   pinch of salt, and a few grinds of pepper. Pour the egg mixture
   into the crust. Top evenly with the pancetta and the shredded
   cheese.

7 Bake the quiche until the eggs are gently set and the top is
   golden, about 25 minutes. Let cool for at least a few minutes
   before cutting into wedges and serving.

You might say I am addicted to poached eggs, which in my opinion make almost any savory dish more delicious. Here, the delicate whites and runny yolks add a touch of luxury to crunchy frisée coated with hot bacon dressing. This is a piece of classic French cuisine I can enjoy anytime. My girlfriends adore it for brunch.

Frisée Salad with Poached Eggs & Bacon Dressing

1   Put the frisée and escarole in a large bowl.

2   Put a large (approximately 10-inch) skillet over medium-low heat. Add the bacon and cook until golden brown and a little crispy, about 8 minutes. Add the shallot, reduce the heat to low, and cook until softened, about 2 minutes.

3   To poach the eggs, put a 1½-quart saucepan over medium heat and add water to reach about halfway up the sides. Bring to a simmer and stir in the distilled white vinegar.

4   One at a time, break the eggs into a small bowl and carefully tip them into the gently simmering water. When all four eggs are in, turn off the heat, cover the pan, and set a timer for 3½ minutes for runny yolks, 5 minutes for firmer ones.

5   While the eggs poach, add the red wine vinegar, mustard, and parsley to the skillet with the bacon. Cook over medium-high heat until bubbly, about 1 minute. Scrape all of the bacon mixture over the frisée and toss to coat evenly. Divide the salad among 4 plates.

6   When the eggs are ready, remove them, one at a time, with a slotted spoon, gently dabbing them with a kitchen towel to soak up excess water, and put 1 egg on top of each salad. Sprinkle the tops lightly with salt and pepper, and top with the chives.

1 head frisée (curly endive), cleaned and trimmed, cut into bite-size pieces (about 4 cups)

1 small head escarole, cleaned and trimmed, cut into bite-size pieces (about 4 cups)

4 ounces thick-cut bacon, cut into ½-inch dice

1 shallot, finely minced

1½ tablespoons distilled white vinegar

4 large eggs

2 tablespoons red wine vinegar

1 teaspoon whole-grain mustard

1 tablespoon finely chopped flat-leaf parsley

Salt and freshly ground black pepper

2 tablespoons finely chopped fresh chives

This favorite breakfast dish is a bit like *mozzarella en carrozza* (an Italian version of grilled cheese) meets soufflé. Much of the work can be done ahead, and it feeds an army. Just mix it up the night before and it's ready to bake in the morning for a special breakfast or brunch.

Savory Bread Pudding

2 tablespoons olive oil, plus more for the pan

1 small yellow onion, cut into ½-inch dice

1 cup cherry tomatoes, halved, or quartered if large

Salt and freshly ground black pepper

2 teaspoons Italian seasoning, homemade (page 14) or store-bought

2 tablespoons coarsely chopped fresh basil

1 sourdough baguette

6 large eggs

1¾ cups whole milk

¼ cup heavy cream

8 ounces whole milk mozzarella cheese, finely chopped

½ cup freshly grated Parmigiano-Reggiano

1 teaspoon salt

1 Put a large (approximately 10-inch) skillet over medium heat. Add the oil and let it get hot. Add the onion and cook until it is translucent and begins to develop a bit of color, 5 to 7 minutes. Add the tomatoes. Season with a bit of salt, pepper, and the Italian seasoning, and cook until the tomatoes cook down slightly, a few minutes more. Stir in the basil. Remove from the heat.

2 Oil a 9 × 13-inch baking dish. Tear the bread into 1-inch chunks and put them into the pan.

3 In a bowl, whisk together the eggs, milk, and cream. Stir in the mozzarella, parmigiano, salt, and the tomato mixture. Pour the egg mixture over the bread, cover with foil, and refrigerate for at least 6 hours or overnight.

4 Preheat the oven to 350°F.

5 Bake the bread pudding, covered, for 45 minutes. Remove the foil and bake until the top is puffed and golden brown, 30 to 40 minutes longer.

6 Cut into wedges, and serve immediately.

One day, while baking Cheddar-bacon scones, it occurred to me that the same combination would make a fabulous waffle. The next day, I tried these out on friends (for dinner—because I was so impatient!). After the first bite, the room went silent. The combination of salty bacon and sweet maple syrup is a sure bet. Add an extra layer of flavor from sharp Cheddar cheese and the crunch of waffles, and it's no wonder these were such a hit.

Cheddar-Bacon Waffles

1   In a bowl, mix together the flour, baking powder, sugar, and salt. Mix in the Cheddar, bacon, and chives.

2   In a separate bowl, whisk together the milk, eggs, and melted butter. Pour into the flour mixture and stir with a wooden spoon or spatula until just combined. Let stand for a few minutes while you prepare the waffle maker.

3   Preheat a nonstick waffle maker. Cook the batter in batches following the instructions for the waffle maker. Serve right away, with syrup. Arrange leftover waffles in a single layer on a baking sheet and freeze. Once frozen, pack the waffles into a resealable freezer bag and freeze for up to 2 weeks. To eat, toast as many waffles as you wish directly from the freezer in a toaster or toaster oven until warm and crisp.

2 cups all-purpose flour

1½ tablespoons baking powder

1 tablespoon sugar

½ teaspoon salt

2 cups shredded extra-sharp Cheddar cheese

5 slices bacon, cooked until crispy and crumbled

2 tablespoons finely chopped fresh chives

1½ cups whole milk

2 large eggs

8 tablespoons (1 stick) unsalted butter, melted

Maple syrup, warmed

I make a batch of these muffins on a Sunday afternoon, so I can grab one for a quick breakfast or snack all week. When shopping for bananas, I buy a few extras and leave them out to get very ripe, just so I can make these tasty treats. Admittedly, overripe bananas don't make the most elegant centerpiece for my table, but that doesn't bother me: the uglier the bananas, the more delicious the muffins!

Banana-Walnut Muffins

1⅔ cups all-purpose flour

½ cup walnuts, toasted and coarsely chopped

1 teaspoon baking powder

½ teaspoon baking soda

½ teaspoon ground cinnamon

¼ teaspoon salt

5 tablespoons unsalted butter, softened

⅓ cup sugar

2 large eggs

1 cup mashed bananas (about 3 medium bananas)

1 teaspoon pure vanilla extract

1 Preheat the oven to 400°F. Line a 12-cup muffin tin with liners.

2 Measure out the flour into a mixing bowl. Spoon out 3 tablespoons of the flour into a small bowl and add the nuts, stirring to coat the nuts with flour.

3 Whisk the baking powder, baking soda, cinnamon, and salt into the bowl with the remaining flour.

4 In the bowl of a stand mixer fitted with the paddle attachment, mix the butter and sugar at medium speed until light and creamy, about 2 minutes. Add the eggs and mix 1 minute longer. Mix in the bananas and vanilla until well combined.

5 Stir the flour mixture into the butter mixture just to incorporate everything. Fold in the walnuts, along with any flour remaining in the bowl.

6 Use an ice cream scoop to divide the batter evenly among the wells of the muffin tin. Bake until a toothpick inserted into the center of a muffin comes out clean, about 18 minutes. Let the muffins cool in the pan for 5 minutes, then transfer them to a wire rack to cool completely.

7 Store leftover muffins in an airtight container at room temperature for up to 3 days.

I was about twelve years old when I came across a cinnamon roll for the first time. I was in a Pennsylvania mall, and it was right after I had moved from Italy to America. The cinnamon scent was alluring, and the roll was topped with a kind of cream cheese frosting I'd never eaten before. After that first encounter, I insisted we go to that mall every weekend, just so I could have another roll, always ordered with extra frosting. As I've grown older, I realize that homemade is far better than store-bought, which has only heightened my obsession!

Cinnamon Rolls

1   Make the dough: Put the warm water into a small bowl, stir in 1 teaspoon of the granulated sugar, and sprinkle the yeast over the top. Let stand for 5 minutes.

2   In the bowl of a stand mixer fitted with the dough hook, at medium-low speed, mix the egg, milk, salt, vanilla, ¼ cup of the melted butter, the remaining ¼ cup granulated sugar, and the yeast mixture. Add 2 cups of the flour and mix until everything is incorporated. Gradually add the remaining 2 cups of flour. Increase the speed to medium and mix until a smooth dough forms, 5 to 7 minutes.

3   Oil a large bowl. Turn the dough out of the mixer and form it with your hands into a ball. Put the dough in the prepared bowl, turning it to lightly coat the dough all over with the oil. Cover with plastic wrap and put in a warm spot to rise until doubled in volume, 1½ to 2 hours.

4   Punch down the dough and roll it out on a floured surface into a 9 × 15-inch rectangle.

(recipe continues)

DOUGH

¼ cup warm water (110°F to 115°F)

¼ cup plus 1 teaspoon granulated sugar

1 (¼-ounce) packet active dry yeast

1 large egg

¾ cup whole milk

1 teaspoon salt

¼ teaspoon pure vanilla extract

8 tablespoons (1 stick) unsalted butter, melted

4 cups all-purpose flour

Safflower oil

FILLING

5 tablespoons unsalted butter, softened, plus more for the pan

¾ cup (packed) light brown sugar

¼ cup granulated sugar

1½ tablespoons ground cinnamon

GLAZE

4 tablespoons cream cheese, softened

1 tablespoon unsalted butter, softened

1¼ cups confectioners' sugar

½ teaspoon pure vanilla extract

3 to 4 tablespoons warm milk

5   Add the filling: Spread the softened butter evenly over the entire surface of the dough. In a small bowl, mix together the brown sugar, granulated sugar, and cinnamon; sprinkle evenly over the dough.

6   Generously butter a 9 × 13-inch baking pan.

7   Position the dough with a long end facing you and brush the far long end with a bit of water. Roll up the dough into a log, starting from the close end, keeping it as tight as you can. Press the end to seal.

8   Use a sharp knife to cut the log crosswise into 1-inch segments, making 14 rolls. Arrange the rolls with a cut side down in the prepared pan. Cover with plastic wrap and let rise in a warm spot until doubled in volume, about 1½ hours.

9   In the last 20 minutes of rising, preheat the oven to 350°F. Just before baking, brush the tops of the rolls with the remaining ¼ cup melted butter. Bake until the rolls are golden brown, about 25 minutes. Set aside to cool slightly.

10   Make the glaze: In a small bowl, stir together the cream cheese, butter, confectioners' sugar, and vanilla. Stir in the milk, about a tablespoon at a time, until the glaze is a pourable consistency.

11   Drizzle the glaze over the tops of the cinnamon rolls, and serve warm.

These doughnuts are a staple in my nonna's kitchen and nearly always make an appearance on Sunday mornings, when overnight guests awaken. Using cooked potatoes as the base is the secret to these doughnuts' crisp, golden exterior and buttery soft interior, making my nonna's doughnuts the best in all of Bacoli.

Homemade Italian Doughnuts

2 teaspoons active dry yeast

¼ cup milk, warmed

2 cups all-purpose flour, plus more for kneading

2 cups plus ¼ cup sugar

1 large egg

1½ cups mashed (boiled and peeled) Yukon Gold potatoes (about 3 medium)

2 tablespoons (¼ stick) unsalted butter, softened

1 teaspoon pure vanilla extract

Finely grated zest of 1 small lemon

½ teaspoon salt

2 tablespoons limoncello (optional)

Safflower oil

1   In a small bowl, stir the yeast into the warm milk; set aside for 5 minutes.

2   In a large bowl, mix together the flour, ¼ cup of the sugar, the egg, potatoes, butter, vanilla, lemon zest, salt, and limoncello, if using. Stir in the milk-and-yeast mixture and mix to form a sticky dough.

3   Turn the dough out onto a well-floured surface and knead until it is smooth and no longer sticky, about 10 minutes, adding a bit more flour, if needed.

4   Line a baking sheet with parchment paper and sprinkle lightly with flour.

5   Cut the dough into 18 reasonably equal pieces. Roll each piece into an 8-inch-long rope, then pinch the ends together to form a circle. As you form them, transfer the doughnuts to the prepared baking sheet. When you have formed them all, cover the doughnuts with a kitchen towel and let rise in a warm spot until they have doubled in volume, about 1 hour 15 minutes.

6   To fry the doughnuts, fill a large Dutch oven halfway full with oil and heat until the oil reaches 375°F. (Put the handle end of a wooden spoon into the oil; if the oil bubbles vigorously around the handle, it's ready.) Line a plate with paper towels and put it near the stove. Put the remaining 2 cups sugar in a shallow bowl.

7 Carefully slide in the doughnuts, one at a time, without crowding them, cooking them in batches of about 4 at a time, depending on the size of your pot. Cook until golden brown on the bottom, about 1 minute, then turn and cook until golden on the second side, about 1 minute longer. Transfer the doughnuts to the prepared plate to drain as they are ready.

8 After draining briefly, dip the hot doughnuts into the sugar on both sides and transfer to a serving platter. These are best when they are hot, so dig in!

9 Store leftover doughnuts in an airtight container at room temperature for up to 2 days.

If you like pancakes and popovers, you will love this Dutch baby, which shares the best qualities of both. Essentially a pancake batter that's baked rather than griddled, this baby puffs up dramatically in the oven, then falls back into a wonderfully eggy pancake. Serving a Dutch baby always makes me look like a rock star, and it will you, too. I recommend a dollop of mascarpone cream on top to seal the deal.

Dutch Baby with Lemon Mascarpone & Berries

1 Make the Dutch baby: Preheat the oven to 400°F with a 9-inch round metal cake pan on the oven rack. Wait 15 minutes for the oven to heat before preparing the batter.

2 Process the flour, sugar, salt, warm milk, eggs, lemon zest, and vanilla in a food processor or blender until smooth.

3 Put the butter into the preheated pan and return the pan to the oven until the butter is melted, 30 to 40 seconds. Pour the batter into the center of the hot pan and bake for exactly 25 minutes without opening the oven door.

4 Slide the Dutch baby onto a wire rack and let cool completely, about 10 minutes.

5 Make the mascarpone cream: Using a chilled bowl and beaters, whip the cream until firm peaks form.

6 In a separate bowl, use a wooden spoon or spatula to mix together the mascarpone, confectioners' sugar, lemon zest, and vanilla. Fold the whipped cream into the mascarpone mixture until evenly combined.

7 Serve the Dutch baby cut into wedges, topped with the cream, fresh berries, and a little lemon zest.

DUTCH BABY

½ cup all-purpose flour

2 tablespoons granulated sugar

Pinch of salt

⅔ cup warm whole milk (110°F to 115°F)

2 large eggs

½ teaspoon grated lemon zest

½ teaspoon vanilla bean paste or pure vanilla extract

2 tablespoons (¼ stick) unsalted butter

MASCARPONE CREAM

½ cup heavy cream

¼ cup mascarpone, softened

2 tablespoons confectioners' sugar

1 teaspoon grated lemon zest

½ teaspoon pure vanilla extract

1½ cups fresh blueberries

Though pancakes are simple to make and require only basic pantry items, the ingredients and technique make all the difference. In this recipe, I use buttermilk for remarkably soft, fluffy cakes. I like to change up the chips from time to time, substituting butterscotch or peanut butter chips or, around the holidays, spiced pumpkin pie chips. No matter which chips strike your fancy, after trying these, you will never pick up a box of packaged pancake mix again.

Fluffy Chocolate Chip Pancakes

1⅓ cups all-purpose flour

¼ cup sugar

2 teaspoons baking powder

1 teaspoon baking soda

½ teaspoon salt

1¾ cups buttermilk

2 large egg yolks

3 tablespoons unsalted butter, melted, plus more for the pan

1 teaspoon pure vanilla extract

2 large egg whites

1 cup semisweet chocolate chips

1 In a large bowl, stir together the flour, sugar, baking powder, baking soda, and salt.

2 In a small bowl, whisk together the buttermilk, egg yolks, butter, and vanilla.

3 In a small bowl, using a handheld electric mixer, beat the egg whites until firm peaks form.

4 Fold the buttermilk mixture into the flour mixture until just combined. Gently fold in the egg whites, until they are slightly streaky. Let the batter rest for 5 minutes.

5 Preheat a griddle pan or nonstick skillet over medium heat and brush it with a little butter.

6 Ladle the batter onto the hot griddle in batches, using about ½ cup per pancake. Sprinkle a generous tablespoon of chocolate chips over the surface of each pancake.

7 Cook until little bubbles form all over the surface of the pancakes, 1 to 2 minutes, then flip and cook until cooked through, 1 to 2 minutes more.

8 Serve straight from the griddle, or cover with foil to keep warm for up to 20 minutes before serving.

Scones are one of my favorite things to bake for a large gathering. Meyer lemon—believed to be a cross between lemons and mandarin oranges—gives these a bright, sweet-tangy flavor. If you can't find them in your area, either lemon or orange makes a good substitute for both the zest and juice. These scones are even better when you prepare them the night before, covering and refrigerating the dough on the baking sheets, ready to bake in the morning. (Brush them with the egg wash when you're ready to bake them.)

Meyer Lemon–Blueberry Scones

SCONES

2¼ cups all-purpose flour

⅓ cup sugar

1½ teaspoons baking powder

¼ teaspoon baking soda

½ teaspoon salt

8 tablespoons (1 stick) cold unsalted butter, cut into ½-inch pieces

2 large eggs

½ cup plus 1 tablespoon half-and-half

½ teaspoon vanilla bean paste or pure vanilla extract

Finely grated zest of 1 Meyer lemon

¾ cup dried blueberries

GLAZE

2 cups confectioners' sugar

1 tablespoon fresh Meyer lemon juice

½ teaspoon vanilla bean paste or pure vanilla extract

Up to 3 tablespoons whole milk

1 Make the scones: Preheat the oven to 400°F. Line a baking sheet with parchment paper.

2 In the bowl of a stand mixer fitted with the paddle attachment, mix the flour, sugar, baking powder, baking soda, and salt briefly to combine. Add the cold butter and mix until it has just broken up a bit and is distributed evenly throughout the flour mixture.

3 In a small bowl, whisk together 1 of the eggs, ½ cup of the half-and-half, the vanilla, and lemon zest. Mix into the flour mixture on low speed until the dough just comes together around the paddle. Mix in the blueberries just long enough to incorporate them.

4 Turn the dough out onto a lightly floured work surface and shape into an 8-inch round. Cut the dough in half, then quarters, then cut each piece in half again to make 8 wedge-shaped scones. Transfer the scones to the prepared baking sheet, leaving about 1½ inches between them.

5 Beat the remaining egg with the remaining 1 tablespoon half-and-half. Brush the tops of the scones with the egg wash. Bake the scones until they are golden brown, 18 to 20 minutes. Let cool completely on a wire rack.

6 Mix the glaze: Stir together the sugar, lemon juice, and vanilla.
   Gradually stir in just enough milk to create a creamy-runny
   consistency.

7 Drizzle the glaze over the scones and let set for at least
   30 minutes before serving.

8 Store leftover scones in an airtight container at room
   temperature for up to 2 days, or refrigerate for up to 5 days.

ACKNOWLEDGMENTS

To my amazing team at Clarkson Potter, thank you for this opportunity, and for helping me to turn my dream into reality. I've wanted to write a cookbook for as long as I can remember, and it's been a pleasure doing it with you! Thanks to Rica Allannic, Stephanie Huntwork, La Tricia Watford, Michael Nagin, Terry Deal, Luisa Francavilla, Anna Mintz, Natasha Martin, Carly Gorga, Lauren Velazquez, Doris Cooper, and Aaron Wehner.

A big thank-you to Jennie Schacht for helping me put my voice on paper and for making the writing process a real joy. Without you this book would have been six hundred pages long, because we both know I can't stop talking or writing. I'm so thankful to have done this with you!

This book would not be so gorgeous without the magnificent Lucy Shaeffer behind the lens. A true artist with a passion for authentic photographs, you captured my food and style perfectly and made the shoot such fun. Thanks to the amazing styling of Carrie Purcell and Paige Hicks, the book is more beautiful than I could have imagined. Thank you for bringing my vision to life!

To my agents—Jon Rosen, Megan Mackenzie, and Eric Lupfer—thanks for always having my back and guiding me in the right direction. Special thanks to Eric for introducing me to Rica and Potter. I feel incredibly lucky to have worked with you all!

To my friends and family, thank you for being patient when I wouldn't leave the kitchen for months while creating, testing, and writing recipes. Thank you for ditching your weekend plans, and instead coming to my kitchen to taste. A huge thank-you to Melissa Vaughan and Irma Schreiber for your long days and nights of recipe testing. You two kitchen rock stars made me feel so comfortable throughout the whole process, and I'm thrilled the recipes have your stamp of approval!

To my viewers, this book would not have been possible without you. Thank you for allowing me to live my dream, and for traveling on this journey with me. You are the heart of my kitchen!

To my parents, thank you for teaching me the value of being myself without apology. You have both been role models in this regard, and I've admired your confidence as long as I can remember. Thank you for teaching me that an occasional slice of cake for breakfast is good for the soul.

To my nonna, there are no words to describe how thankful I am for you. You've taught me how to work hard, love unconditionally, and live authentically. I admire your lifelong love of food and desire to feed those you love, and I'm honored to share this passion with you. *Ti voglio un mondo di bene, nonnina mia!*

Finally, my dear Joe, thank you for always believing in me, and for singlehandedly building me a kitchen where I can cook and bake all day and share my passion with people everywhere. You are my biggest dream come true.

INDEX

Note: Page references in *italics* indicate photographs.

A

Apple Danish, 199
Apple Toffee Crumble, *158,* 159

B

Bacon
   Breakfast Bruschetta, *210,* 211
   -Cheddar Waffles, *222,* 223
   Dressing & Poached Eggs, Frisée
      Salad with, *218,* 219
   One-Pan Eggy Breakfast, 208, *209*
   Pancetta & Fontina Quiche, 216–17,
      217
   & Red Cabbage Slaw, 122, *122*
   Spaghetti Carbonara, 44, *45*
Banana-Walnut Muffins, 224
Basil Pesto, 15, *15*
Bean(s)
   Black, Spicy, 123
   Breakfast Quesadillas, 214
   Cannellini, with Pancetta & Spinach,
      134, *135*
   Cornbread Dumpling–Topped Chili,
      98–99, *99*
   Pasta e Fagioli, 50
   Pasta with Chickpeas, *42,* 43
   & Rice Enchiladas, 100
Beef
   Ciabatta Steak Sandwich with
      Arugula, *28,* 29
   Cornbread Dumpling–Topped Chili,
      98–99, *99*
   Filet of, au Poivre, *112,* 113
   Gorgeous Bolognese, *76,* 77
   Greek Meatballs in Pita, 26–27, *27*
   Grilled Flank Steak with Chimichurri,
      64, 65
   Mama's Italian Meat Loaf, 115
   Meat & Three-Cheese Lasagne, *84,*
      85–86
   Nonna's Stuffed Peppers, 106–7, *107*
   Pasta Genovese, 73
   Pasta with Braised Short Ribs, 87–88,
      89
   & Pastina Soup, The Ultimate Italian,
      74–75, *75*
   Pot Roast alla Pizzaiola, 114

Speedy Weeknight Cheeseburgers, 30
Beets, Balsamic Roasted, 130, *131*
Blackberry Jam Oat Bars, *188,* 189
Blini with Smoked Salmon & Scrambled
   Eggs, 206–7, *207*
Blueberry(ies)
   Dutch Baby with Lemon Mascarpone &
      Berries, *230,* 231
   –Meyer Lemon Scones, 234–35, *235*
   Stunning Pavlova, *172,* 173–74
Bread Puddings
   Orange–Vanilla Bean, 153
   Savory, 220, *221*
Breads
   Banana-Walnut Muffins, 224
   Breakfast Bruschetta, *210,* 211
   Cinnamon Rolls, 225–26, *227*
   Cranberry Rolls, *196,* 197–98
   Garlic, Cheesy, 146, *147*
   Garlicky Bruschetta, 58, *59*
   Meyer Lemon–Blueberry Scones,
      234–35, *235*
Bread salads
   Fattoush with Grilled Chicken, 24–25,
      25
   Panzanella Salad, 120, *121*
Broccoli
   Mac & Cheese Bake, The Cheesiest
      Ever, 90–91, *91*
   White Veggie Pizza, 93–95

C

Cabbage, Red, & Bacon Slaw, 122, *122*
Cakes
   Devil's Food, Devilishly Good, 170–71,
      171
   Mama's Babà al Rum, 176–77, *177*
   Red Velvet Cupcakes, 175
   Yellow, with Raspberry Jam & Orange
      Whipped Cream, *148,* 160–61
Carrots, Cumin-Roasted, 142, *142*
Cauliflower Stufato, 136
Cheese
   Breakfast Quesadillas, 214
   Broccoli Mac & , Bake, The Cheesiest
      Ever, 90–91, *91*
   Cheddar-Bacon Waffles, *222,* 223

Cheesy Garlic Bread, 146, *147*
Classic Margherita & White Veggie
   Pizza, *68,* 93–95
Eggplant Parm Bake, 104–5
Goat, & Pesto–Stuffed Chicken
   Breasts, 51
No-Bake Nutella Cheesecake, *168,* 169
Pancetta & Fontina Quiche, 216–17,
   217
Parmesan-Roasted Potato Halves, 132
Pasta al Forno with Vegetable Sugo,
   78–79, *79*
Savory Bread Pudding, 220, *221*
Spaghetti Cacio e Pepe, 31
Speedy Weeknight Cheeseburgers, 30
Spinach & Artichoke–Stuffed Shells,
   82–83, *83*
Three- , & Meat Lasagne, *84,* 85–86
Tortellini with Pink Parmesan Sauce,
   38, 39
Cherry-Chocolate Puddings, 152
Chicken
   Breasts, Pesto & Goat Cheese–
      Stuffed, 51
   Grilled, Fattoush with, 24–25, *25*
   Herbes de Provence Roasted, 110, *111*
   One-Pan, with Potatoes, Wine &
      Olives, 62, *63*
   Paella, *96,* 97
   Roasted, Cacciatore, *108,* 109
   & Root Vegetable Casserole, Biscuit-
      Topped, 101–3, *102*
   Sausages with Black Lentils, 52, *53*
Chili, Cornbread Dumpling–Topped,
   98–99, *99*
Chocolate
   & Caramel Shortbread Tart, 166–67,
      167
   -Cherry Puddings, 152
   Chip Pancakes, Fluffy, 232, *233*
   Dipping Sauce, Churros with, 162–63
   Fudgy Brownies, *192,* 193
   Mocha Meringues, 186, *187*
   No-Bake Nutella Cheesecake, *168,* 169
Churros with Chocolate Dipping Sauce,
   162–63
Cinnamon Rolls, 225–26, *227*

Coffee
  Hazelnut Tiramisù, *164, 165*
  Mocha Meringues, 186, *187*
Cookies & bars
  Blackberry Jam Oat Bars, *188,* 189
  Butterscotch Blondies, 190, *191*
  Fig Jam Cookies, 184
  Fudgy Brownies, *192, 193*
  Granola & Dried Fruit Bars, 185
  Lemon Almond Biscotti, *180,* 182–83
  Mocha Meringues, 186, *187*
Corn & Clam Chowder, 70–71, *71*
Cranberry Rolls, *196,* 197–98
Crème Brûlée, Jammy, 150–51, *151*
Cupcakes, Red Velvet, 175

D

Doughnuts, Homemade Italian, 228–29, *229*
Dutch Baby with Lemon Mascarpone & Berries, *230,* 231

E

Eggplant
  Parm Bake, 104–5
  Pasta alla Norma with Sausage Meatballs, 40–41, *41*
Eggs
  Baked, 205
  Benedict, Italian, 212–13, *213*
  Breakfast Bruschetta, *210,* 211
  Breakfast Quesadillas, 214
  Mama's Italian Meat Loaf, 115
  One-Pan Eggy Breakfast, 208, *209*
  Poached, & Bacon Dressing, Frisée Salad with, *218,* 219
  Scrambled, & Smoked Salmon, Blini with, 206–7, *207*
  Spaghetti Carbonara, 44, *45*
Enchiladas, Rice & Bean, 100

F

Fennel & Orange Salad, 126, *127*
Fig Jam Cookies, 184
Fish
  Blini with Smoked Salmon & Scrambled Eggs, 206–7, *207*
  Cakes, Crispy, with Tartar Sauce, 56–57
  Calamari Puttanesca, 36, *37*
  Halibut Saltimbocca, *54,* 55

Pasta Shells with No-Cook Tuna Sauce, *34,* 35
  Quinoa Salad with Poached Salmon, *46, 47*
Frisée Salad with Poached Eggs & Bacon Dressing, *218,* 219
Fruit. *See also specific fruits*
  Dried, & Granola Bars, 185
  Salad, Orange-Scented, with Honey Yogurt, *202,* 203
  Stunning Pavlova, *172,* 173–74

G

Garlic
  Bread, Cheesy, 146, *147*
  Garlicky Bruschetta, 58, *59*
  Roasted, Polenta, *144,* 145
  -Stuffed Pork Loin, 116, *117*
Granola, Maple Nutty, 204
Granola & Dried Fruit Bars, 185

H

Ham
  Halibut Saltimbocca, *54,* 55
  Italian Eggs Benedict, 212–13, *213*
  Peas, & Gorgonzola, Bow-Tie Pasta with, 32, *33*

K

Kale, Mint & Radish Salad, *124,* 125

L

Lemon
  Almond Biscotti, *180,* 182–83
  Citrus Meringue Pie, 155–56, *157*
  Meyer, –Blueberry Scones, 234–35, *235*
Lentils, Black, Sausages with, 52, *53*

M

Meatballs, Greek, in Pita, 26–27, *27*
Meat Loaf, Mama's Italian, 115
Meringue(s)
  Mocha, 186, *187*
  Pie, Citrus, 155–56, *157*
  Stunning Pavlova, *172,* 173–74
Muffins, Banana-Walnut, 224
Mushroom(s)
  Marsala, 137, *137*
  Ragù, Tagliatelle with, *80,* 81

N

Noodles, Creamy Buttery, 143
Nuts
  Granola & Dried Fruit Bars, 185
  Hazelnut Tiramisù, *164,* 165
  Lemon Almond Biscotti, *180,* 182–83
  Maple Nutty Granola, 204
  No-Bake Nutella Cheesecake, *168,* 169

O

Oat(s)
  Bars, Blackberry Jam, *188,* 189
  Granola & Dried Fruit Bars, 185
  Maple Nutty Granola, 204
  Toffee Apple Crumble, *158,* 159
Orange
  Citrus Meringue Pie, 155–56, *157*
  & Fennel Salad, 126, *127*
  –Vanilla Bean Bread Pudding, 153

P

Pancakes, Fluffy Chocolate Chip, 232, *233*
Pantry basics, 10–11
Pasta
  al Forno with Vegetable Sugo, 78–79, *79*
  alla Norma with Sausage Meatballs, 40–41, *41*
  Bow-Tie, with Peas, Ham & Gorgonzola, 32, *33*
  with Braised Short Ribs, 87–88, *89*
  Calamari Puttanesca, 36, *37*
  The Cheesiest Ever Broccoli Mac & Cheese Bake, 90–91, *91*
  with Chickpeas, *42,* 43
  e Fagioli, 50
  Genovese, 73
  Gorgeous Bolognese, *76,* 77
  Meat & Three-Cheese Lasagne, *84,* 85–86
  Shells with No-Cook Tuna Sauce, *34,* 35
  Spaghetti Cacio e Pepe, 31
  Spaghetti Carbonara, 44, *45*
  Spinach & Artichoke–Stuffed Shells, 82–83, *83*
  Tagliatelle with Mushroom Ragù, *80,* 81
  Tortellini with Pink Parmesan Sauce, *38,* 39

The Ultimate Italian Beef & Pastina
    Soup, 74–75, *75*
Peach Melba, *178*, 179
Pea(s)
    Ham, & Gorgonzola, Bow-Tie Pasta
        with, 32, *33*
    Salad, Minty, *128*, 129
Pepper(s)
    & Potato Hash, 215
    Stuffed, Nonna's, 106–7, *107*
Pesto, Basil, 15, *15*
Pie, Citrus Meringue, 155–56, *157*
Pizza, Classic Margherita & White
    Veggie, *68*, 93–95
Polenta, Roasted Garlic, *144*, 145
Pomegranate Eton Mess, 154, *154*
Pork. *See also* Bacon; Ham
    Chops alla Milanese, 66, *67*
    Gorgeous Bolognese, 76, *77*
    Loin, Garlic-Stuffed, 116, *117*
    Meat & Three-Cheese Lasagne, *84*,
        85–86
    Pasta alla Norma with Sausage
        Meatballs, 40–41, *41*
    Sausage & Clams with Tomatoes,
        60, 61
Potato(es)
    Halves, Parmesan-Roasted, 132
    & Pepper Hash, 215
    Shortcut Crispy Old Bay Fries, *138*,
        139
    Wine, & Olives, One-Pan Chicken with,
        62, *63*
Puddings
    Bread, Orange–Vanilla Bean, 153
    Bread, Savory, 220, *221*
    Cherry-Chocolate, 152
Pumpkin Pie Spice Twists, 194, *195*

Q
Quiche, Pancetta & Fontina, 216–17, *217*
Quinoa Salad with Poached Salmon,
    46, 47

R
Radish, Kale & Mint Salad, *124*, 125
Raspberries
    Peach Melba, *178*, 179
    Stunning Pavlova, *172*, 173–74

Rice
    & Bean Enchiladas, 100
    Mock Risotto with Pesto & Turkey
        Marinara, 48, *49*
    Nonna's Stuffed Peppers, 106–7, *107*
    Paella, *96*, 97
    Wild, Pilaf, 140, *141*

S
Salads
    Fattoush with Grilled Chicken, 24–25,
        25
    Fennel & Orange, 126, *127*
    Frisée, with Poached Eggs & Bacon
        Dressing, *218*, 219
    Kale, Mint & Radish, *124*, 125
    Orange-Scented Fruit, with Honey
        Yogurt, *202*, 203
    Panzanella, 120, *121*
    Pea, Minty, *128*, 129
    Quinoa, with Poached Salmon, *46*, 47
Sauces
    Basil Pesto, 15, *15*
    Chocolate Dipping, Churros with,
        162–63
    Gorgeous Bolognese, 76, 77
    Marinara, 13
Sausage(s)
    with Black Lentils, 52, *53*
    & Clams with Tomatoes, *60*, 61
    Meatballs, Pasta alla Norma with,
        40–41, *41*
    Meat & Three-Cheese Lasagne, *84*,
        85–86
Scones, Meyer Lemon–Blueberry,
    234–35, *235*
Seasoning, Italian, 14, *14*
Shellfish
    Clam & Corn Chowder, 70–71, *71*
    Crispy Fish Cakes with Tartar Sauce,
        56–57
    Paella, *96*, 97
    Sausage & Clams with Tomatoes,
        60, 61
    White Wine Mussels with Garlicky
        Bruschetta, 58, *59*

Slaw, Red Cabbage & Bacon, 122, *122*
Soups
    Beef & Pastina, The Ultimate Italian,
        74–75, *75*
    Butternut Squash, Easy, with Crisp
        Sage Leaves, *22*, 23
    Clam & Corn Chowder, 70–71, *71*
    Split Pea, Slow-Simmered, 72
    Tomato, Fresh, 20, *21*
    Weeknight Minestrone, *18*, 19
Spinach
    & Artichoke–Stuffed Shells, 82–83, *83*
    & Pancetta, Cannellini Beans with,
        134, *135*
    White Veggie Pizza, 93–95
Split Pea Soup, Slow-Simmered, 72
Squash
    Butternut, Soup, Easy, with Crisp
        Sage Leaves, *22*, 23
    Sautéed Garlic & Lemon Zucchini,
        118, 133

T
Tart, Caramel & Chocolate Shortbread,
    166–67, *167*
Tomato(es)
    Classic Margherita Pizza, *68*, 93–95
    Marinara Sauce, 13
    Passata, 13
    Soup, Fresh, 20, *21*
Turkey Marinara & Pesto, Mock Risotto
    with, 48, *49*

V
Vegetable(s). *See also specific vegetables*
    Root, & Chicken Casserole, Biscuit-
        Topped, 101–3, *102*
    Weeknight Minestrone, *18*, 19

W
Waffles, Cheddar-Bacon, *222*, 223
Wild Rice Pilaf, 140, *141*

Z
Zucchini, Sautéed Garlic & Lemon, *118*,
    133

CONVERSION CHART

Equivalent Imperial & Metric Measurements

American cooks use standard containers, the 8-ounce cup and a tablespoon that takes exactly 16 level fillings to fill that cup level. Measuring by cup makes it very difficult to give weight equivalents, as a cup of densely packed butter will weigh considerably more than a cup of flour. The easiest way therefore to deal with cup measurements in recipes is to take the amount by volume rather than by weight. Thus the equation reads:

1 cup = 240 ml = 8 fl. oz.   ½ cup = 120 ml = 4 fl. oz.

It is possible to buy a set of American cup measures in major stohres around the world.

In the States, butter is often measured in sticks. One stick is the equivalent of 8 tablespoons. One tablespoon of butter is therefore the equivalent to ½ ounce / 15 grams.

LIQUID MEASURES

Fluid Ounces	U.S.	Imperial	Milliliters
	1 teaspoon	1 teaspoon	5
⅓	teaspoons	1 dessertspoon	10
½	1 tablespoon	1 tablespoon	14
1	2 tablespoons	2 tablespoons	28
2	¼ cup	4 tablespoons	56
4	½ cup		120
5		¼ pint or 1 gill	140
6	¾ cup		170
8	1 cup		240
9			250, ¼ liter
10	1¼ cups	½ pint	280
12	1½ cups		340
15		¾ pint	420
16	2 cups		450
18	2¼ cups		500, ½ liter
20	2½ cups	1 pint	560
24	3 cups		675
25		1¼ pints	700
27	3½ cups		750
30	3¾ cups	1½ pints	840
32	4 cups or		900
	1 quart		
35		1¾ pints	980
36	4½ cups		1000, 1 liter
40	5 cups	2 pints or 1 quart	1120

SOLID MEASURES

U.S. and Imperial Measures		Metric Measures	
Ounces	Pounds	Grams	Kilos
1	¾ cup	28	
2	1 cup	56	
3½		100	
4	1¼ cups	112	
5	1½ cups	140	
6		168	
8	2 cups	225	
9	2¼ cups	250	¼
12	2½ cups	340	
16	3 cups	450	
18		500	½
20	3½ cups	560	
24	3¾ cups	675	
27	4 cups or	750	¾
28	1 quart	780	
32		900	
36	4½ cups	1000	1
40	5 cups	1100	
48		1350	
54		1500	1½

OVEN TEMPERATURE EQUIVALENTS

Fahrenheit	Celsius	Gas Mark	Description
225	110	¼	Cool
250	130	½	
275	140	1	Very Slow
300	150	2	
325	170	3	Slow
350	180	4	Moderate
375	190	5	
400	200	6	Moderately Hot
425	220	7	Fairly Hot
450	230	8	Hot
475	240	9	Very Hot
500	250	10	Extremely Hot

Any broiling recipes can be used with the grill or the oven, but beware of high-temperature grills.